D0464189

Twayne's English Authors Series

Sylvia E. Bowman, *Editor*

INDIANA UNIVERSITY

Arthur Symons

 76

Arthur Symons

By JOHN M. MUNRO

The American University of Beirut, Lebanon

Twayne Publishers, Inc.   ::   New York

LIBRARY
WAYNE STATE COLLEGE
WAYNE, NEBRASKA

Copyright © 1969 by Twayne Publishers, Inc.
All Rights Reserved

Library of Congress Catalog Card Number: 68–17234

MANUFACTURED IN THE UNITED STATES OF AMERICA

For Ingrid

113790

Preface

It is still widely believed that English literature of the past hundred years can be conveniently divided into two periods of significant achievement separated by a decade or so of trivia and mediocrity. The first period, usually dated from around the accession of Queen Victoria in 1837, is dominated by the poet Tennyson and ends a few years before the laureate's death in 1892. The second supposedly begins some time before World War I with the dramatic appearance of T. S. Eliot and Ezra Pound, who, it is believed, were almost entirely responsible for creating that literature which we call "modern." The years between, loosely referred to as the 1890's, are generally regarded as an interlude, as a time when certain minor writers with greater talent for showmanship than literature appeared briefly, then conveniently disappeared, died or went mad, leaving the stage free for greater figures.

This impulse to submerge the significance of the 1890's between the twin promontories of Victorian and modern literature can perhaps be justified in terms of the quality of the work produced during the middle period, but to isolate these years from the continuity of the literary tradition in an effort to establish evidence for either a decline in the Victorian sensibility, or, more rarely, an indication that greater things were to come, is to suggest that literary history is more conveniently schematic than we have a right to expect it to be.

It is not surprising, therefore, that there has been a recent tendency to view the literature of the past two hundred years in terms of a single tradition which, for want of a better name, we may call "Romantic." In this context, the 1890's have assumed a role more transitional than apocalyptic, and are now regarded as a time when the existing tradition was modified rather than radically altered. With this change of perspective, there has been a correspondent shift of emphasis; and it is now less likely that the 1890's are remembered only for the shocking perversities of Oscar Wilde's *Salome* or the languorous cadences of Ernest Dowson's *Cynara,* than they are for the significant implications of the esthetic of Walter Pater and the far-reaching effects of the introduction of French Symbolism.

This change of view has also meant a revision in critical estimates of some of the central figures of the 1890's and perhaps no one has benefited more than Arthur Symons. Until fairly recently Symons was regarded quite simply as the Decadent *par excellence;* as a delicate hot-house poet who chronicled the pains and tribulations of love; an Impressionist critic who melted before the melancholy cadences of Verlaine and who trembled exquisitely before the Satanic enormities of Baudelaire. Indeed, many believed that he had faded with the nineteenth century—together with Audrey Beardsley, Dowson, Lionel Johnson, and Oscar Wilde —and were no doubt surprised to learn of his death in 1945. Others, aware of his survival into the twentieth century, seem to have regarded his death as little more than the belated departure of a literary anachronism. Richard Jennings, for example, acknowledged his passing in *The New Statesman* on February 17, 1945, with these words:

Last month died—physically, officially, notifiably—Arthur Symons, born in 1865: poet, dramatist, impressionist traveler, eager enquirer into the theory and practice of what it pleased him to enumerate the "seven arts": the arts of literature, music, painting, sculpture, architecture, handicraft, dancing and the stage. I make them eight; but it does not matter. It is, however, important to note that the indefatigable writer who in 1886 produced a slim volume on Browning which Browning tried to dissuade him from writing, the associate of all the "Ninety-ish" poets and critics of the Rhymers' Club, the too faithful disciple of Walter Pater, the friend and companion of George Moore and W. B. Yeats, died mentally—or to all creative effort—in 1908. Thereafter, all that was published under his name must be "received with caution."

Jennings' reference to 1908 as the end of Symons' career as an effective writer is not questioned, for in that year Symons suffered his mental breakdown. It is true that he recovered sufficiently to resume his interrupted literary career, but the quality of his later work is vastly inferior to that which he had written earlier, and it is all too clear that, after 1908, Symons was only in imperfect control of his faculties.

Jennings' facetious disparagement of his earlier achievement, however, is quite unacceptable. Before 1908 Symons had been regarded by his contemporaries as one of the foremost critics of his day and as a poet of considerable talent if somewhat limited range. Furthermore, his importance is not confined to the 1890's; for, as Frank Kermode has recently suggested in *Romantic Image*, Symons is a "crucial" figure in relation to the development of the English poetical tradition, a writer whose achievement needs to be understood before one can properly appreciate the essential characteristics of the modern esthetic.

Although some may find Symons' original work rather tiresome in its self-conscious display of period naughtiness, and his criticism irritatingly vague, his total achievement has considerable historical significance. In his writings we can trace the development of the modern esthetic from Walter Pater and Robert Browning through the French Symbolists to T. S. Eliot, Ezra Pound and James Joyce; and, if nothing else, Symons' literary career effectively demonstrates that the notion of the 1890's as a break in the English literary tradition is quite untenable. Therefore, I am less concerned in this study with examining Symons' achievement as a writer than with establishing his importance as an influence. Nevertheless, I have endeavored to show that Symons' work merits more sympathetic consideration than it usually receives, both for its qualities as literature and also as the expression of a fascinating, tortured, and at times pathetic figure, who came to realize how dearly the sincere artist must pay for his vision.

JOHN M. MUNRO

American University of Beirut

Acknowledgments

The present volume is based on a doctoral dissertation submitted to the Department of English at Washington University, St. Louis, in 1962. Professor Leon Gottfried was then my adviser, and to him I owe a great debt for his patient and good-natured guidance. To the Universities of North Carolina and Toronto I am also indebted: to the former for a research grant which enabled me to spend two profitable weeks among the Symons' papers at Princeton University in 1962, and to the latter for generous aid in the preparation of the typescript.

I am also grateful to a number of publishers for allowing me to quote material for which they hold the copyright. In particular I would like to thank Messrs. Secker and Warburg for permission to quote from Symons' poetry in the *Collected Works*, but my thanks are also due to Constable and Co. for allowing me to publish a lengthy extract from *Spiritual Adventures*; to the Bodley Head Ltd. for permission to quote from *Charles Baudelaire: A Study* and *Baudelaire: Prose and Poetry*; to E. P. Dutton and Co. Inc. for allowing me to publish two long pieces from their recent reprint of *The Symbolist Movement in Literature*; to C. W. Beaumont for permission to print a passage from Symons' *The Café Royal and Other Essays*; to Bobbs-Merrill and Co. Inc. for permission to reprint a passage from *Dramatis Personae*.

I would also like to express my gratitude to the New York Public Library for allowing me to publish a letter from Rhoda Symons to W. B. Yeats. To the Princeton University Library I owe a particularly large debt for allowing me access to the Symons papers in its possession and for granting me permission to quote extensively from them. Finally, to my wife, who had nothing to do with either the composition of the book or with the preparation of the typescript, yet without whom this study would never have been written, I owe my deepest debt of gratitude. It is to her that this volume is dedicated.

Contents

Chronology

1865   February 21, Arthur Symons born at Milford Haven, Wales; son of an itinerant Wesleyan preacher.

1886   Published his first important work, *An Introduction to the Study of Browning*, which, together with his article on *Frédéric Mistral* in the *National Review*, and his participation in the editing of the Shakespeare Quarto Facsimiles, under the direction of Dr. Furnivall, brought him to the attention of many important literary figures of the time.

1888   Met Pater at Oxford, two years after they had first exchanged letters.

1889   Made the first of many trips to the Continent in the company of Havelock Ellis; he met such major French writers of the 1890's as Mallarmé, Huysmans, Remy de Gourmont, Henri de Régnier. Published his first volume of poems, *Days and Nights*, dedicated to Pater; he and Browning were the two main influences on his early literary development. A convenient date to mark the end of Symons' "Victorian" period and the beginning of his "Decadent" period.

1890   April 29, met Verlaine, who was to become a major influence in his subsequent development. Began to write poetry which clearly reflected the Frenchman's influence.

1891   Joined the Rhymers' Club where he first came into contact with W. B. Yeats, who was to become a close friend during the latter part of the 1890's.

1892   *Silhouettes*, his first typically Decadent volume of poems.

1893   Verlaine visited England to give a series of lectures organized for him by Symons, William Rothenstein, and Professor Frederick York-Powell of Oxford. Symons published *The Decadent Movement in Literature*, thus establishing himself as the spokesman for the English Decadence.

1894   Met Lydia, a dancer from the Empire, who exercised a profound fascination over Symons until his death.

1896 A crucial year in Symons' development. Broke with Lydia; but unable to free himself from the memory of her. Visited Ireland with Yeats, now a close friend. Met Aubrey Beardsley, with whom he edited *The Savoy.* The approximate beginning of Symons' Symbolist phase.

1898 Met Rhoda Bowser, whom he married in 1901. Engaged in an increasing amount of literary journalism to make financial provision for his forthcoming marriage.

1899 Published *The Symbolist Movement in Literature,* his most important work. This book impressed such people as T. S. Eliot, Ezra Pound, and James Joyce, all of whom were influenced by Symons' account of the Symbolist esthetic, adapting it to their own special needs.

1902 Extended tour of Europe and the Baltic countries with Rhoda. Yeats introduced Joyce to Symons. Symons began to write more extensively on subjects other than literature and the theater.

1903 Published *Plays, Acting and Music,* in which he applied his understanding of the Symbolist esthetic to the theater and music, and *Cities,* a collection of travel sketches.

1906 *Studies in Seven Arts,* in which he applied the Symbolist esthetic to criticism of all the arts.

1908 Mental breakdown while vacationing in Italy; confined in a mental institution.

1910 Partially recovered sanity; retired to his cottage in Kent; remained there until death.

1911 Met Joseph Conrad, on whom he wrote appreciative essay in 1907 which remained unpublished until 1923, when it was included in *Dramatis Personae.*

1919 Regained some of his old working rhythm. Produced many volumes of criticism and verse but unable to approximate his earlier achievements.

1920 Published his first book-length study of Baudelaire.

1936 November 3, death of Rhoda after a long illness.

1945 January 22, death of Symons. Buried in the churchyard at Wittersham, Kent, his home for almost forty years.

CHAPTER 1

Arthur Symons: Victorian

I *Influence of Pater and Browning*

FOR many years Walter Pater's historical significance rested solely on the rather dubious distinction of his influence on the men of the 1890's, particularly Oscar Wilde. Frank Harris, for example, in his colorful and highly untrustworthy biography of Wilde, records the spiritual kinship which he feels existed between the two men; and he refers to an incident which is supposed to have taken place on the banks of the river Cherwell where Pater and Wilde were sitting, watching the students bathing, "the beautiful white figures all grace and ease and virile strength." Apparently Wilde spoke as if inspired of how Christianity had flowered into romance, how the pale Christ had been outlived, and how the world was moving towards a synthesis of art in the ideals of a new paganism which would combine romantic beauty and Classicism.

Then, in a pause in the conversation, Pater, "the stiff, quiet, silent Pater," moved beyond the expression of words, suddenly slipped from his seat, knelt down beside Wilde and planted a devotional kiss on his hand.[1]

A few years later, T. S. Eliot complained that "the degradation of philosophy and religion, skilfully initiated by Arnold, is competently continued by Pater," and that "his view of art, as expressed in *The Renaissance*, impressed itself upon a number of writers in the 'nineties, and propagated some confusion between life and art which is not wholly irresponsible for some untidy lives." [2]

Certainly Pater's influence on the 1890's in general, and on Wilde in particular, is beyond dispute, as Wilde's review of *Appreciations*,[3] the Paterian echoes in his *The Picture of Dorian Gray*,[4] and his acknowledgment of his debt to Pater in *De Profundis*[5] all testify. In recent years, however, it has been customary to maintain that Wilde distorted Pater to suit his own special needs, or perhaps quite innocently failed to understand his origi-

17

nal intentions.[6] Thus, although Pater speaks at length about the necessity of multiplying and intensifying one's sensations,[7] he does not insist that these sensations should be valued for their own sake.

On the contrary, their importance lies less in themselves than in their function of providing insight into truth.[8] Therefore, when Pater affirms the primacy of art because it "comes to you proposing frankly to give nothing but the highest quality to your moments as they pass, and simply for those moments' sake,"[9] he is not making a simple plea of "art for art's sake" in the commonly held meaning of that phrase. Instead, he is re-affirming Plato's belief in the inseparableness of beauty and goodness. Art intensifies one's responses and heightens one's sensibility; and, because in Pater's view one's sensibilities provide insight into moral knowledge, art itself is the only true morality.[10] Hence "burning with a hard gem-like flame" is not a rather refined species of spiritual orgasm, a private experience between a thing of beauty and a sensitive spectator, or an intense emotional act that is final in itself. To Pater, every work of art was a means of communication, and its ultimate human value was its power to widen man's moral sensibilities, to yield "quickened and multiplied consciousness," and so, without direct didactic intent, to provide a final guide to conduct.

The ethical implications of Pater's esthetic were either misunderstood or ignored by Wilde, who seems to have felt that Pater was advocating merely the cultivation of the sensations for their own sake; and, when Wilde wrote in *The Picture of Dorian Gray* that "one could never pay too high a price for any sensation,"[11] he was thinking only in terms of the experience itself. Pater was not slow to point out Wilde's mistake, and in a review of the novel he noted that "a true Epicureanism aims at a complete though harmonious development of man's entire organism," and in no way implied a loss of "moral sense."[12] Later, recognizing where his admirers may have been led astray, Pater suppressed the conclusion to the second edition of *The Renaissance*, because it "might mislead some of the young men into whose hands it might fall,"[13] and perhaps a similar fear prompted him to omit his essay on "Aesthetic Poetry" in the second edition of *Appreciations*.[14]

Symons could not have been one of the misled young men whom Pater had in mind, for the second edition of *The Renais-*

sance had appeared in 1877; and Symons and Pater did not become acquainted before 1886.[15] Nevertheless, Symons was in some respects the kind of person who could have been led astray. Born into a strict Methodist family at Milford Haven, Wales, in 1865, the son of an itinerant Wesleyan preacher, Symons' early years were spent largely in the West Country, where he was reared by a pious, rather distant father and by an equally pious, but more approachable, mother. Although at the age of thirteen he composed an exemplary religious poem entitled "A Dream of the Garden of God," he soon came to view his parents' fervid religiosity with distaste; and, although tormented with thoughts of hell and damnation, he found it quite impossible to reconcile himself to the kind of God about whom his parents so earnestly spoke.[16]

As the dream of God's garden faded, Apollo's became increasingly luminous. Symons loved to read; he also liked music; and these became for him a welcome escape from the tedium of his pious, middle-class existence. Inevitably, it was the music of Chopin which made a deep, early impression upon him; and soon he was also enjoying a "guilty delight in reading books which told him about the sensations of physical love."[17] With no religious faith to stabilize him and with a temperament both morbid and sensitive, it is hardly surprising that he soon became an enthusiastic admirer of Pater.

At first, however, Symons does not seem to have been aware that Pater might offer him a code of life which would replace the religious faith he had lost. Primarily, he seems to have used him as a model for his prose style; but he also responded to what Graham Hough has called "the Paterian temperament."[18] In May, 1885, for example, Symons wrote to Churchill Osborne, the young schoolteacher and freelance journalist to whom Symons looked for guidance during his early years, to inform him that the style of an article he had written on the Provençal poet, Frédéric Mistral, was inspired by Pater, whom even at this time Symons describes as "the most exquisite [critic] of the day."[19] A year later, in his first significant publication, an edition of *Venus and Adonis* for Frederick Furnivall's Shakespeare Quarto reprint series, Symons left little doubt about his stylistic master when he concluded his introduction with these words: "The chambers of the House of Life are not of an even whiteness, the pure unbroken whiteness of whitewash; they are coloured with diverse colours, they are hung with the arras woven of dreams and deeds, and the picturings upon the walls of the chambers of the House of Life are many." [20]

In the preface Symons wrote for the Mermaid edition of *The Best Plays of Philip Massinger,* Pater's influence is equally apparent when Symons writes that in Massinger's poetry there is "such intrinsic and unmistakable beauty that we are forced to pause and brood on them with the true epicure's relish." [21] In his introduction to a collection of Leigh Hunt's essays, Pater's presence may be detected when Symons states that in Hunt's company "we are travellers in enchanted places," in "the Garden of Eden," and in "The House Beautiful," and that his fine writing is "practically flawless and rounded." Furthermore, his remark that Hunt sees not with a painter's eye, but as one for whom beauty is everything, is reminiscent of Pater's introduction to *The Renaissance,* in which he sets forth his esthetic credo.[22] Introducing the plays of John Day, Symons finds the main charm of the dramatist to lie in his delicate perception of the transience of earthly things; and he notes that in his plays "gentle and petulant figures come and go like figures in a masque, aimlessly enough, yet to measure," while the total effect of Day's work is to provide an "escape" which frees the reader from all "the disabilities of our never quite satisfied existence." [23] In short, in all Symons' early work the influence of the master is not in doubt; and there is considerable justification for Jennings' labeling him "the too faithful disciple of Walter Pater."

Nevertheless, one should be wary of taking Jennings' remark too literally, for it is doubtful whether Symons was fully aware, at this stage of his career, of the complexities of Pater's esthetic. In an essay which appeared as late as 1896, Symons found Pater's two most significant qualities to be his sensitive discrimination of beauty and his delicate, voluptuous prose style. Nowhere is there a suggestion that Symons had deduced from Pater either the kind of debased hedonism which Wilde extrapolated from him, or the ethical code based on esthetic appreciation which Pater evidently intended.[24]

In his essay, Symons expresses his admiration for Pater's style by applying to him lines which Pater himself had used to describe Charles Lamb,[25] concluding that not only had Pater raised criticism to a fine art, but had expressed himself in a prose "which made the splendour of Ruskin seem gaudy, the neatness of Matthew Arnold a mincing neatness, and the brass sound strident in the orchestra of Carlyle." [26] Finally, Symons, making his approval of Pater's style even clearer, and in this instance making quite explicit his affection for Pater's Decadent charm, goes on to praise *The Renaissance* by calling it "the most beautiful book of prose in our literature" and by pointing to the "almost oppressive quiet, a quiet which seems to exhale the atmosphere heavy with the odour of tropical flowers" which broods over its pages.[27]

There is little doubt that Symons became saturated in his early years with Pater, attempting to reproduce the involutions of his prose style and laying himself open to "all impressions," and doing what he could to bring about "a more intimate sympathy with some of the subtler aspects of art." [28] On the whole, Pater's influence was salutary, once Symons had learned to avoid the preciosity, which, for example, had marred the conclusion to his introduction to *Venus and Adonis*. Thus, in his first major critical study, *An Introduction to the Study of Robert Browning*, Symons achieves a more personal style, although Pater's mark is still apparent. He also analyzes Browning's poetry in some detail, avoiding what he referred to, in 1896, as Pater's "speculations before a canvas, a literary fantasy; a possible interpretation, if you will, of one mood of the painter, a single side of his intention," a characteristic of the master he found both irritating and limiting.[29]

Symons had been interested in Browning for some time before he wrote his *Study*. Indeed, he later admitted that, if Pater had exercised the most powerful influence on his early prose, he was equally indebted to Browning for influencing his early verse.[30] At the age of sixteen, Symons had joined the Browning Society at the time of its inception; and, almost from the beginning, he had played an active part. In 1882 we find him telling Churchill Osborne of his correspondence with Furnivall concerning a poem published in an American newspaper which he felt had been wrongly attributed to Browning, and exulting over the receipt of a letter from the poet himself, disclaiming all responsibility for its composition.[31] He presented a number of papers to the society before 1885, and it was perhaps inevitable that he should have tried his hand at a full length study of the poet, which eventually appeared in 1886.[32]

Here again, although perhaps not quite so clearly, Pater's prose style has left its mark. In this instance, however, Symons has managed to avoid the more obvious stylistic idiosyncrasies of Pater; he has combined good sense and decorative detail without sacrificing his own artistic integrity on the gilt and purple altar of Pater's rococo sensibility. James Dykes Campbell was probably responsible for restraining Symons' stylistic exuberance; for, as Symons acknowledged elsewhere, the older man had "been at [his] elbow all the time" during the composition of the Browning study, and had "rigorously shorn" a number of his "most eloquent passages," and "severely straightened" some "pet eccentricities of phrase." [33] Consequently, the places where Symons leans towards extravagance are rare. Once, perhaps, when comparing Browning's landscapes to "sabre-strokes, swift, sudden, flashing the light from their sweep, and striking straight to the heart . . . never pushed into prominence for an effect of idle beauty, nor strewn about in the way of thoughtful and passionate utterance like roses in a runner's path," we can detect Pater's influence.[34] And in speaking of "Rabbi Ben Ezra" as a "light through the darkness—a lantern of guidance, and a beacon of hope—to the wanderers lost and weary in the *selva selvaggia*," there is also the faint shadow of the master.[35] On the whole, however, such stylistic indulgences are rare; and, for the most part, Symons writes in an admittedly "poetic" style, but one which is not embarrassingly obtrusive.

More significant, however, is a passage in which Symons links the names of both Pater and Browning, giving a clear indication of the direction his personal esthetic would develop. He tells us that Browning's practice is "to reveal the soul to itself" by "a sudden test, which shall condense the long trial of years into a single moment, and so 'flash the truth out by one blow.'" Browning selects a character, writes Symons, "and places it in some situation where its vital essence may become apparent—in some crisis of conflict or opportunity," and he goes on to quote Pater, indicating that Pater's ideal is also Browning's: "To realise such a situation, to define in a chill and empty atmosphere the focus where rays, in themselves pale and impotent, unite and begin to burn, the artist has to employ the most cunning detail, to complicate and refine upon thought and passion a thousand fold. . . . Yet, in spite of this intricacy . . . we receive from it the impression of one

imaginative tone, of a single creative act." [36] In other words, both
Pater and Browning were concerned with the same thing: to isolate the significant moment; and, by contemplating it, to penetrate
to the very essence of a character or situation.[37]

II Days and Nights

The extent to which this isolation and penetration became
Symons' aim also is particularly clear from his first published volume of poetry, *Days and Nights* (1889), a collection of verses
written between 1884 and 1888, and dedicated to Pater.[38] The
titles Symons gave to these poems are indicative of his aim: "An
Interruption in Court," "An Episode Under the Nihilists," "An Act
of Mercy," "Magdalen at the Threshold," "Satiety," "Red Bredbury's End," "The Temptation of St. Anthony," and "Episode of a
Night in May." Unlike Pater, who deals almost exclusively with
souls of rarefied sensibility, but, like Browning, who—so Symons
had written—"dealt with or touched on nearly every phase and
feature of humanity," Symons tells us not to seek art ". . . on
some far peak/. The home of clouds, the sanctuary of stars"; but
to

> . . . go where the cities pour
> Their turbid human stream through street and mart,
> A dark stream flowing onward evermore
> Down to an unknown ocean;—there is Art.

On the other hand, Symons does not share the general optimism
which is supposedly characteristic of Browning—what Symons
had called in his study of the poet, his "cheeriness of intellectual
health." Instead, he leans more towards the melancholy Pater, insisting that, as Man's life is not particularly joyful, Art has a responsibility to sing "less of Days than Nights." [39]

Indeed, the poems of *Days and Nights* are all rather gloomy.
They deal with women who have been betrayed; with the distressing plight of the poor and their struggle for survival in a
crass, mercenary world; with females who have been forced into
lives of sin. Yet, in spite of these obviously distressing themes, the
poems themselves hardly move one at all. A dramatic interlude
entitled "An Episode Under the Nihilists," is typical, a poem
which hardly gains from its association, whether intentional or

not, with Wilde's ranting melodrama, *Vera*.[40] In Symons' poem, Dmitri has slain Vassili for the "cause"; Vera, the murderer's wife, hears of it; and then she suddenly realizes that Vassili meant more to her than her husband. At the end of the poem she discovers that she actually despises Dmitri and vows never to speak to him or to love him again. As a psychological study the poem is deficient, for Symons' Vera and Dmitri are as wooden as Wilde's characters of the same names; and their passion is of the melodramatic sort, neither subtle nor real, nor, indeed, very interesting. As a result, the poem fails to move, in spite of the violence of Vera's denunciation and the impassioned cynicism of Dmitri's reply; what emotion there is in the poem is hollow, theatrical, and really rather ridiculous.

In fact, all the poems in this collection are marred by a similar falseness. In, for example, the maudlin "Interruption in Court," a garrulous and tearful father pleads for his daughter charged with prostitution;[41] or, to cite another typical example, in "A Home Circle," a mother sits by a dying fire awaiting the return of her drunken husband.[42] Perhaps the most excruciating excursion into sentimentality, however, is "A Café Singer," which could almost be a parody of Browning written by an inferior poet of the Spasmodic school; but it is actually an obviously derivative version of an inept poem by Robert Louis Stevenson.[43] A dying child, the daughter of a café singer, pleads with her mother not to work so she can be with her while she dies. Unfortunately, the mother goes to work, but on her return the child is still alive and has strength enough to carry on a halting conversation before she finally expires, affirming at the end, however, that God will understand, even though mother and daughter have found it impossible to prepare for the child's departure with prayer.

Admittedly, "A Café Singer" is perhaps an extreme example of Symons' weakness as a poet, but its faults are typical of the whole volume. The trouble is that the moments of crisis in nearly all the poems are too obviously contrived, and depend for their effect on a naturalistic setting, which is particularly unfortunate, as Symons has not the power to make us accept as real the contexts in which these moments of intensity occur. Instead, they recall the sentimental paintings so much in vogue at the time, whose overstrained pathos moves one to laughter rather than to tears. Thus, though Symons seems to have attempted to crystalize a series of dramatic situations and to make them symbols of the human condition, he rarely succeeds.

One of the reasons for Symons' lack of success is his too obvious dependence on literary sources. Almost all the poems in *Days and Nights* seem to have been inspired by literary models rather than real-life situations; and, although most of the poems are cast in dramatic form, one feels the poet has a certain facility for imitating Browning rather than an acute ear for conversation and a perceptive insight into human psychology. Indeed, Browning's influence is everywhere apparent, most notably in the extensive use of the dramatic monologue, but sometimes Symons owes a debt to specific poems. "Red Bredbury's End," for example, recalls "The Bishop Orders His Tomb at St. Praxed's Church"; "A Revenge" seems to owe something to Browning's "My Last Duchess"; and in "A Vigil in Lent" Symons makes use of a lover's whistle to call his mistress, a dramatic device which Browning had used in "Andrea del Sarto." [44] Other influences seem to be Théophile Gautier, whose poem "L'Art," Symons echoes in "Venus of Melos," and to whom he makes direct acknowledgement in "Posthumous Coquetry"; William Blake, whose theory of the "mundane shell" he alludes to in "A Crisis," and whose influence seems to lie behind "Of Charity"; Henri Murger, Heinrich Heine, Villiers de l'Isle Adam, Joachim du Bellay and Catullus, to all of whom he specifically acknowledges his indebtedness; and, finally, Dante Gabriel Rossetti, Coventry Patmore, George Meredith, Robert Louis Stevenson, and Charles Baudelaire.

The life that Symons describes in these poems is seen consistently through a literary man's spectacles. Pater himself, in a generally enthusiastic review noted this quality; but he approved because, he wrote, Symons goes to the literature "which is most in touch with the actual life around us." [45] Unfortunately, whatever realism and vitality may have been in Symons' sources, surprisingly little of it has come into his own writing, and, as a result, we rarely feel involved in the situations the poet describes.

That the detached and withdrawn Pater should have admired these poems, calling them "concentrations, powerful, dramatic, of what we might call the light and shadow of life," [46] is not perhaps surprising, and, although we feel inclined to reverse almost every judgment he made with regard to individual poems, he does, nevertheless, draw our attention to that aspect of Symons' poetic talent which was to produce some of his most effective work. Pater first complains that "the complex, perhaps too matterful, soul of our century has found in Mr. Browning and some other excellent modern English poets, the capacity for dealing masterfully with it, excepting only that it has been too much for their perfect lucidity of mind, or at least of style." But, he says, in Symons "the rich poetic vintage of our time has run clear at last"; for his poems are lucid without being simple-minded.[47] Lucid the poems of *Days and Nights* certainly are; and, although Symons was to move on to describe some of the more complex areas of human experience, he managed to retain clarity of expression. Nevertheless, as far as *Days and Nights* is concerned, what has been gained in "lucidity" has usually been at the expense of substance; and the result is that Symons' "rich poetic vintage" is really a rather flavorless, watered-down Browning.

However, in one or two places, Symons does seem to break away, partially at least, from his literary models, and to write something which seems to have been inspired by a genuinely felt human emotion. Such a poem is "A Crisis." [48] In this piece the narrator, plagued with insomnia, finds himself in a dream world of phallic pine trees, pursued by a nameless horror:

> One persistent thought
> Panted behind, and urged him on: he turned
> And faced his foe.
> In a scattered flash of lights,
> Leaping, and whirled, and mixed inextricably,
> The fiery letters of a deadly sin
> Stood out before him. All beside was vague.
> He could remember nothing. Am I mad,
> He wondered, or indeed this criminal?
> He strove to think, but as he strove his mind
> Faltered, all shone, lights danced before his brain,
> The ground rose up before him, swayed, fell back,
> He reeled, and caught both hands against a pine.
> There glowed the letters and the fiery act:
> He gazed on them with horror.

At this point, however, "the spectre" is still at bay; but at last he triumphs, and the poet surrenders himself to the full wrath of God:

> all his soul
> Shuddered within him at the wrath of God,
> The anger of the outraged Lawgiver,
> Pealed in a voice from Sinai; bare he stood
> To every arrow flaming down from the skies,
> The witness and the avenger. "Strike!" he cried:
> A burst of blazing fire filled all the air:
> And then the madness took him; while the storm
> Howled in the heights and tossed the deeps to light,
> Hurling the cataracts of the clouds abroad
> And running down the hills of heaven in flame.

Although one can discern in this poem the influence of Blake, and possibly also of Shelley's "Alastor," it seems likely that Symons was primarily concerned with dramatizing a dream, similar in nature, although not quite so extreme, to those he later described in the autobiographical first chapter of *Spiritual Adventures*. These were nightmares in which he was made to climb a series of "infinite spirals," or ladders whose rungs dropped away from him as he ascended; or sometimes to descend "slimy stone stairways into cold pits of darkness"; horrible dreams in which he could feel the tightening of a snake's coil around him, or in which he imagined he was walking "with bare feet across a floor curdling with snakes." [49]

One does not need to know much Freud to sense the obvious sexual significance of such psychical manifestations, and Symons himself stated that, during his childhood, he was exceedingly susceptible to "dreams of abstract horror" into which began to come "a disturbing element of sex." [50] Soon Symons became ashamed of his desires; he felt guilty after reading books which described sensations of physical love; and inevitably he came to look upon sex and evil as synonymous. This conjunction of physical passion and sinfulness remained with Symons beyond adolescence, and it is perhaps not too much to say that his inability to recognize that sexual enjoyment did not necessarily mean damnation was an important factor in his subsequent mental breakdown.

The personal note which is struck in "A Crisis," however, is not typical of the poems in *Days and Nights*. Most of the verses in this volume are little more than literary exercises, and many of them could have been written by anyone with a modicum of sensibility and an aptitude for rhyme. Occasionally Symons impresses us as a more than competent metrist, indicating that, although he was perhaps somewhat callow in both the choice and treatment of his subject matter, he was a metrical craftsman of considerable maturity. The variety of poetical forms he uses is in itself astonishing, and a few of his poems are both deft and accomplished, as for example, "The Street Singer," [51] where Symons manages to transcend the banality of a commonplace subject, at the same time revealing considerable sophistication in his handling of the sonnet form.

But Symons had not yet found his own poetic voice, and there is little indication that he was likely to become England's most eloquent spokesman on behalf of the Decadent ideal. The last poem in the collection, however, does give us a foretaste of what was to come. It is called "The Opium Smoker," and in it Symons evokes the synthetic dreams he imagines the drug would induce:

> I am engulfed and drown deliciously.
> Soft music like a perfume, and sweet light
> Golden with audible odours exquisite,
> Swathe me with the cerements for eternity.
> Time is no more. I pause and yet I flee.
> A million ages wrap me round with night.
> I drain a million ages of delight.
> I hold the future in my memory.

Although the Decadent subject to some degree anticipates the major preoccupations of Symons' next two volumes of verse, *Silhouettes* (1892) and *London Nights* (1895), and although his use of the technique of synesthesia suggests that he has been reading Baudelaire, the sestet of the poem—which draws attention to the moral degradation of the addict—demonstrates that Symons has not yet turned his back on the manse:

> Also I have this garret which I rent,
> This bed of straw, and this that was a chair,
> This worn-out body like a tattered tent,
> This crust, of which the rats have eaten part,
> This pipe of opium; rage, remorse, despair;
> This soul at pawn and this delirious heart.[52]

Thus, even in "The Opium Smoker," Symons is still the provincial, non-conformist moralist, and he still depends on naturalistic techniques to depict the squalor of the scene. As Symons matured, he tended to avoid making pat ethical judgments; and, as he grew more certain of his poetical talents, he also tended to eliminate the programmatic content from his poems and to concentrate instead on communicating amoral visions by means of suggestive rather than explicit detail.

And the change came remarkably quickly. When one compares *Days and Nights* with Symons' next volume, *Silhouettes*, which appeared only three years later, one realizes that in the interval he had become more mature psychologically and technically. Instead of the pretentious, hollow-sounding, obviously derivative pieces which characterized most of the poems of the earlier volume, there are polished, sophisticated little verses, which admittedly deal with a more limited range of subjects, but which nevertheless impress the reader with their deftness and artistry. And, curiously enough, in spite of their artificiality, they seem closer to life. What had happened in between was, briefly, Symons' first trip to France. There he found on the Left Bank a coterie of artists and writers whose bohemianism he found compatible with his own temperament; and, more important, he discovered that their artistic aims were remarkably similar to his own.

CHAPTER 2

Arthur Symons: Decadent

I *Towards a Definition of Decadence*

SYMONS' interest in French literature began early. At fifteen he is known to have translated one of Swinburne's French lyrics and some verses from the Provençal poet Frédéric Mistral, on whom he also wrote a sensitive and appreciative essay in January, 1886; at seventeen, he wrote a poem, "The Defence of Delilah" (never published), supposedly under the influence of Leconte de Lisle; and, of course, in *Days and Nights* he acknowledged the influence of such writers as du Bellay, Villiers de l'Isle Adam, Murger, and Gautier; and a number of the poems in this volume also suggest that he was acquainted with Baudelaire.[1]

However, it was not until 1889 that he made his first trip to Paris, accompanied by Havelock Ellis, with whom he had become closely associated while editing the dramatic works of John Day and Philip Massinger for the Mermaid series, and with whom he later shared rooms in Fountain Court. In Paris they intended not simply "to gaze at the idols of the crowd or to seek out the venerated figures who still survived to enjoy fame won in the generation before," but they hoped instead to meet the leaders of the younger generation: "Mallarmé; Rodin; Verlaine; Huysmans; Carrière; Henri de Régnier; Charles Morice; Odilon-Redon; Remy de Gourmont and others."[2] As it happened, they were unable to see Villiers de l'Isle Adam, who had died the year before; but they were entertained by Verlaine and visited him at his hotel, sat in on one of Mallarmé's famous Tuesday evenings at his house in the Rue de Rome, and were introduced to Huysmans by Remy de Gourmont.[3]

These writers and artists Symons found most congenial; and, although he wrote appreciative essays on such diverse figures as Balzac and Molière, the greater part of his translation and criticism was concerned with the group of writers loosely called "Symbolists," such Romantic writers as Gérard de Nerval, Théophile

Gautier and Petrus Borel—who may be said to have anticipated what the Symbolists did—and the medieval poet, François Villon, who seemed to embody so much that was typical of them.

It is not easy to say what the Symbolists as a group were trying to achieve, but in many aspects they were revolting against prevailing literary conventions. During the early part of the nineteenth century, science had been making new advances, reducing the seemingly miraculous to the commonplace and the concept of evolution in particular had the effect of reducing the stature of man which the Romantics had given him. As a result, these new writers made an attempt to restore his pre-eminence, concentrating attention on his emotions and sensations, those aspects of man which make him unique. Humankind, in general, tended to be ignored in favor of the individual.[4]

With this change of emphasis, it was felt necessary to develop a new poetic language which would be able to register the minute particularities which the poet considered so important. Because these writers believed that ordinary language was useless in rendering the more intricate details of sensation, thought, and feeling, because each moment of consciousness has its own special nuance or flavor, it was felt necessary to transform the language into a special idiom which would adequately convey personality and emotions. And this new idiom was to be intentionally and deliberately "symbolic," for only by suggestion was it felt that one could communicate one's vision.[5]

So it was that poetry, as the Symbolists conceived it, came to be closely associated with music, that art which relies most heavily on evocation and suggestion, "which creates an atmosphere rather than makes a statement."[6] Just what contemporary writers understood by "music" is not always clear, but it seems that there were two distinct points of view.[7] On the one hand, Paul Verlaine evidently thought that poetry should imitate music as closely as possible: the poet should select his words carefully with a view to obtaining a harmonious sound. The concern of Stephane Mallarmé, on the other hand, is less easy to define. While Verlaine evidently thought in terms of audible sound, Mallarmé seems to have conceived it as something perceptible only to the inner ear of the mind—a state of harmony envisaged out of time and out of space, which could only be achieved through the heightened quality of poetic language, "a music of the spheres," as C. M. Bowra has called it, similar to what Pater seems to have had in mind when he insisted that all art constantly aspires to the condition of music.[8]

Finally, as Bowra has also pointed out, the Symbolists were ultimately concerned with mysticism, for their poetry was something of a protest against an age of materialism which had lost its belief in traditional religion; and it was the Symbolists' concern to find an effective substitute.[9] It was, in short, a protest against scientific realism made on behalf of an ideal world, which was, in their estimation, more real than that of the senses, "a religion of ideal beauty, of *le Beau and l'Idéal*." [10]

Although with the benefit of hindsight we can determine in some measure what the Symbolists' aims were, many of their contemporaries, both in France and in England, looked upon them with little sympathy and understanding. In England, George Moore has the distinction of being the first writer to draw attention to them in his garrulous, somewhat exhibitionist *Confessions of a Young Man,* which first appeared in 1888. His remarks there are not, however, very enlightening. He maintains that Symbolism is simply "saying the opposite of what you mean," [11] and he seems, on the whole, far more interested in trumpeting his discovery than in analyzing the Symbolists' aims. Moore followed these early remarks with a longer essay in *Confessions and Opinions* (1891), but it unfortunately adds little more to our understanding of these writers. He contributes one or two colorful anecdotes, promotes what was to become the stereotyped legend of Verlaine as the sweet-singing drunkard amid the sawdust of the Left Bank cafés, and selects for special mention a few faintly perverse and melancholy poems.[12]

In 1893, Edmund Gosse made some sympathetic remarks about Mallarmé, showing an awareness of what he and his contemporaries were trying to achieve; but, at the same time, he considered the sonnets of the Parnassian Hérédia so perfect that "nothing but to withdraw to the wilderness and sheepskins is left to the would-be poets of the next generation." [13] Three years later, still championing the Parnassians at the expense of the Symbolists, he declared, alluding to Gautier's *Emaux et Camées,* "enamel may get to look old-fashioned, but it makes, in the long run, a better show than gelatin." [14]

At first, Symons was also hostile to the new French writers. In 1890, in a short review of Verlaine's "Bonheur," he praised the author highly; but he dissociated him from "the brain-sick little school of Symbolistes" and from "the noisy little school of Décadents."[15] The following year, however, in another article on Verlaine, Symons reprinted almost word for word what he had said about the poet previously; but he omitted the derogatory remarks concerning the two schools.[16] By 1893, Symons seems to have revised his earlier opinion of Verlaine's contemporaries, for in "The Decadent Movement in Literature," he showed considerably more sympathy towards these writers than before.[17] The change in attitude can no doubt be attributed to an increased awareness of their aims, which he would have learned directly from the writers themselves, and certainly from reading Charles Morice's *La Littérature de tout à l'heure*, which, Symons later confessed, "was almost a revelation of a new Gospel."[18]

In any event, Symons' article on the Decadent movement makes a bold attempt to codify the aims and intentions of modern French writers, and to make clear to an unsympathetic public that they were serious artists who deserved respectful consideration. The article was perhaps prompted by an attack on literary decadence by Richard Le Gallienne, a minor poet, essayist, novelist and critic of the period; for in January, 1892, in a review of Churton Collins' *Illustrations of Tennyson*, Le Gallienne had made an effort to "think out the whole question of literary decadence," concluding that it was little more than "limited thinking, often insane thinking."[19] It would be wrong to say that Le Gallienne's definition of Decadence was generally accepted at the time, for few had bothered to analyze the word at all. Usually, the word "Decadent" was bandied about as a term of abuse or tagged to works which seemed to show little respect for prevailing notions of decency and morality. It is not surprising, therefore, that Symons should have come to the defense of Decadence in 1893, making a gallant attempt to define the word more precisely and to give it some literary respectability.

First, he attempts in "The Decadent Movement in Literature" to define the three terms frequently used indiscriminately to characterize the movement—"Decadence," "Symbolism," and "Impressionism." He maintains that Decadence is a general term applied to literature in which there is an "intense self-consciousness, a restless curiosity in research, an over-subtilising refinement upon refinement, a spiritual and moral perversity." It is not a healthy literature, he says. Indeed, it is "typical of a civilisation grown over-luxurious, over-inquiring, too languid for the relief of action, too uncertain for any emphasis in opinion or conduct. It reflects all the moods, all the manners of a sophisticated society; its very artificiality is a way of being true to nature: simplicity, sanity, proportion—the classic qualities—how much do we possess them in our life, in our surroundings, that we should look to find them in our literature—so evidently the literature of a decadence?" [20]

As for Symbolism and Impressionism, they are the two main branches of this kind of literature. Both have much in common; both seek "not general truth merely but *la vérité vraie*, the very essence of truth—the truth of appearance to the senses, of the visible world to the eye that sees it; and the truth of spiritual things to the spiritual vision." However, the Impressionist "would flash upon you in a new, sudden way so exact an image of what you have just seen, just as you have seen it"; and the Symbolist "would flash upon you the soul of that which can be apprehended only by the soul—the finer sense of things unseen, the deeper meaning of things evident." [21]

What Symons meant by this statement is perhaps a little obscure, for his language is certainly vague. However, reference to Symons' poetry of the time does shed some light. In his 1895 volume of poems, *London Nights*, there is a piece called "At Dieppe: Grey and Green," certainly one of his better poems, in which he strives to capture the delicate pastel tones of British Impressionist painter Walter Sickert, and at the same time to communicate in a few words the essence, the "impression," of a scene momentarily observed:

> The grey-green stretch of sandy grass,
> Indefinitely desolate;
> A sea of lead, a sky of slate;
> Already autumn in the air, alas!
>
> One stark monotony of stone,
> The long hotel, acutely white,
> Against the after-sunset light
> Withers grey-green, and takes the grass's tone.

> Listless and endless it outlies,
> And means, to you and me, no more
> Than any pebble on the shore,
> Or this indifferent moment as it dies.[22]

In this poem Symons was concerned merely with describing external nature, "flashing" upon the reader in a "new, sudden way so exact an image of what [he has] just seen, just as [he has] seen it." Thus, "At Dieppe: Grey and Green" may properly be called, at least in Symons' terminology, an "Impressionist" poem.

In "Dawn," however, also included in *London Nights,* and written at about the same time, the focus is on internal nature; and the emotions of the poem's speaker are stimulated by a particular situation:

> Here in the little room
> You sleep the sleep of innocent tired youth,
> While I, in very sooth,
> Tired, and awake beside you in the gloom,
> Watch for the dawn, and feel the morning make
> A loneliness about me for your sake.
>
> You are so young, so fair,
> And such a child, and might have loved so well;
> And now, I cannot tell,
> But surely one might love you anywhere,
> Come to you as a lover, and make bold
> To beg for that which all may buy with gold.
>
> Your sweet, scarce lost, estate
> Of innocence, the candour of your eyes,
> Your childlike, pleased surprise,
> Your patience: these afflict me with a weight
> As of some heavy wrong that I must share
> With God who made, and man who found you, fair.[23]

In a momentary flash of insight, the speaker recognizes something that at other times he might not have been so excruciatingly aware of; in a moment of truth, he sees "the deeper meaning of things evident." Thus in Symons' understanding of the term, "Dawn" is a "Symbolist" poem.

In some respects "Dawn" is somewhat reminiscent of a number

of pieces in *Days and Nights* in which Symons relies on a stock situation and is perhaps needlessly explicit in describing the protagonists' feelings and emotions. He would perhaps have written a better poem had he paid more attention to the criticism of Charles Morice, whose book on contemporary French literature impressed him so much. Morice had objected to Wagner's choice of insufficiently "dreamlike" subjects for his operas, and he had recommended vagueness as an essential ingredient of artistic excellence.[24] As Symons himself recognized, and as he never tired of repeating, he was a man "for whom the visible world exists," [25] and so he was never entirely able to relinquish his hold on the actual and familiar. Consequently, the failure of many of the poems in *Days and Nights* may be attributed to Symons' heavy reliance on naturalistic scene-painting, and also because he had an ingenuous weakness for the overly explicit. As a result, the settings of most of his poems in this book seem more theatrical than real; the events, contrived; and the emotions, stilted. In *Days and Nights,* Symons had not yet mastered the art of suggesting more than he expressed; like Wagner's operas, his early poems lacked the evocative magic of dream.

Symons' preference for the palpable is equally manifest in his attitude to "music" as revealed in "The Decadent Movement in Literature." Charles Morice had upheld the superiority of music over the other arts on account of its vague spirituality. In discussing music however, in Symons' essay, he seems to have had sensuous harmonies in mind and to have favored Verlaine's understanding of the term rather than Mallarmé's. It is hardly surprising, therefore, that Symons preferred the former poet to his now more highly esteemed contemporary; and he credited Verlaine rather than Mallarmé with evolving the poetic language to express the new vision: "Music first of all and before all, he [Verlaine] insists; and then, not colour, but *la nuance,* the last fine shade. Poetry is to be something vague, intangible, evanescent, a winged soul in flight 'toward other skies and other loves.' " [26] Hence, as the ideal of Decadence is "to fix the last fine shade, the quintessence of things; to fix it fleetingly; to be a disembodied voice, and yet the voice of a human soul," [27] Verlaine is great insofar as he came closer than any other poet to attaining this end. Verlaine dealt in palpable harmonies which nonetheless evoked something beyond the senses; he remained firmly rooted in the familiar world—yet looked beyond.

Symons failed to hear Mallarmé's music and, therefore, assumed it did not exist. Hence, to Symons, Mallarmé is a poet of a lower order. It is true that he recognizes his importance in making of "the clear and flowing French language, something irregular, unquiet, expressive, with sudden surprising felicities, with nervous starts and lapses, with new capacities for the exact noting of sensation." But Symons seems to think that Mallarmé went too far, for "alike to the ordinary and the scholarly reader it is painful, intolerable; a jargon; a massacre." So, Symons concludes, Mallarmé's influence must remain personal.[28]

Of the prose writers Symons discusses in "The Decadent Movement in Literature," he recognizes the importance of the Goncourt brothers in making a new prose style to meet the needs of the new literary generation, in much the same way that Verlaine deserved credit for a similar service to poetry.[29] But it is the work of Joris-Karl Huysmans, "so fascinating, so repellent, so instinctively artificial," which represents "the main tendencies, the chief results, of the Decadent Movement in literature." [30] Among the dramatists, Symons chooses not, as one might expect, Villiers de l'Isle Adam, whose *Axel* is usually regarded as the most typical work of the period, but Maurice Maeterlinck, his disciple, whose appeal, Symons finds, is directly to the sensations, and whose "one note" is "fear." [31] Finally, turning to the literature of England, Symons suggests that Pater and W. E. Henley are the most typical representatives of the Decadent movement in England.[32]

That Pater should now be referred to as a Decadent is understandable. Of him, Symons asks rhetorically: *"Marius the Epicurean*, in its study of sensations and ideas (the conjunction was Goncourt's before it was Mr. Pater's), and the *Imaginary Portraits*, in their evocations of the Middle Ages, the age of Watteau —have they not that morbid subtlety of analysis, that morbid curiosity of form, that we have found in the work of the French decadents?" And then Symons goes on to show that Pater is also concerned with isolating those fugitive moments which capture the essence of a particular scene or situation. But the inclusion of Henley into the Decadent band does seem a little odd, for one does not readily associate the poet of "Invictus" with the other

writers Symons discusses in his essay. One can perhaps justify the
Decadent label for Henley on the grounds that, when "The Decadent Movement in Literature" appeared, the poet had not yet
written his aggressively activist verse; and Symons has evidently
based his opinion of Henley on the "In Hospital" sequence and on
"London Voluntaries," both of which are concerned with exploring some of the more morbid aspects of human experience. Nevertheless, Henley's inclusion in the Decadent movement is not
wholly appropriate. It is possible that Symons also thought so
later; for, when his Decadent movement essay was reprinted many
years later, references to both Pater and Henley were excluded.[33]

On the whole, Symons' essay on the Decadent movement is a
satisfactory document. He was perhaps mistaken to have included
Pater and Henley; but, even so, Symons manages to suggest a
certain coherence by observing that the Decadents as a group
were concerned with penetrating to *la vraie vérité* (the very essence of truth), and that they were engaged in distilling the spirit
of a particular scene or aspect of human experience, even though
some of them were less concerned with the curious and the morbid than others. However, in Symons' other literary criticism of
this time he seems to have been drawn to those writers who reveal
not so much a concern with *la vraie vérité* as with a self-conscious
research into the perverse and unsanctified areas of human psychology—writers who in a general way one may call Decadent,
but not in the specific sense Symons had described the term in
discussing Verlaine in his *Harper's Magazine* essay.

Thus, Symons was drawn to Thomas Lovell Beddoes who was
"tired of being merely human," finding him "more amorous of corruption than Beaudelaire," and more "spellbound by the scent of
grave-yard earth than Poe." [34] He writes too of Robert Louis Stevenson who, "in some wonderful artificial way, like a wizard who
raises, not living men from the dead, but the shadows of men who
had once died, calls up certain terrifying but not ungracious phan-
toms, who frisk it among the mere beings of flesh and blood,
bringing with them the strangest 'airs from heaven and blasts
from hell'." [35] He approved of Catulle Mendes, particularly his
La Femme Enfant, where the author's "gracious, flimsy and perverse talent has for once found a subject as gracious, flimsy, and
perverse as itself." [36]

Similarly, Symons devoted an essay to an equally minor English writer, Thomas Gordon Hake, drawing particular attention to his detachment, a quality which he admired in Huysmans. Symons tells us that "never was an English poet more exotic than Dr. Hake," but he emphasizes that this exoticism was not simply a peculiar attitude of mind, a predilection for the perverse and nothing more.[37] Thus, Symons feels justified in suggesting that Hake was in a sense superior to such poets as Baudelaire, Poe, Rossetti, and Swinburne because he had the ability to stand aside from his subject matter, viewing it objectively in an almost impersonal way. Although he appears to favor "morbid themes, he impresses one as being himself no more morbid than the surgeon whom we see eagerly entering a hospital." [38] In this respect Hake differs from James Thompson, another poet of morbid appeal. Thompson believed that in order to "render vulgar life" it was necessary to be vulgar oneself. "He did not realize that to be modern is of all achievements the most difficult, that it requires the most perfect command of oneself and one's material, consummate art; and that here, more than elsewhere, a flaw, a lapse, is fatal alike to the illusion and to the distinction of success." [39]

All these writers have, then, in one way or another, certain Decadent characteristics; but none of them comes so close to the ideal as Symons had described it in "The Decadent Movement in Literature" as Huysmans. Symons had mentioned him briefly in the essay, but he had written more extensively of him elsewhere, pointing out those qualities which make Huysmans so essentially the Decadent prototype, not just in his writing but in his life. Symons recalls meeting him at the house of the "bizarre Madame X," leaning "back on the sofa, rolling a cigarette between his thin, expressive fingers, looking at nothing," lying "back indifferently on the sofa, with the air of one perfectly resigned to the boredom of life." [40] And this detachment from his surroundings, this intellectual aloofness, Huysmans brought to his writings. He did not become involved with the hero of *A Rebours*, but stood apart, concentrating his energies in describing the events of his life as dispassionately and effectively as he could. Thus, he devoted as much attention to *how* he said something as to *what* he actually said. Symons, who recognizes this characteristic of Huysmans, notices too that his style is intensely personal and that "the sense of rhythm is entirely dominated by the sense of colour." [41] He also comments on the high-handed violence Huysmans did to the syntax of the language: "the barbaric profusion" of words and the looseness of construction which helped him describe things as no one had ever described them before.[42] As for the subject matter, Symons notes that Huysmans' psychology was chiefly a matter of sensations, there being in his writings a complete disregard of moral nature. Finally, although unwilling to commit himself as to the quality of *A Rebours* as a whole, Symons does concede that, in spite of its "strangeness and charm" even "repulsion," the work is undoubtedly "the expression of a personality as remarkable as that of any contemporary writer's." [43]

II *Discipleship of Verlaine*

The years between the publication of *Days and Nights* (1889) and *London Nights* (1895) may properly be referred to as Symons' Decadent period. This was the time when he was most strongly attracted by literature characterized by "an intense self-consciousness, a restless curiosity in research, an over-subtilising refinement upon refinement, a spiritual and moral perversity." In his personal life also, Symons went in earnest pursuit of experience, following a course similar to that of des Esseintes: he sought new sensations with avid intellectual curiosity rather than because of a pathological inclination. He entered into a series of love affairs with a variety of women, noting the quality and texture of his experiences without ever wholly giving himself to them;[44] he experimented, cautiously, with hashish;[45] he sought out artists with what must have been an irritating enthusiasm, but, as much, it seems, for the experience of being in their presence as for the opportunity of talking to them about their work;[46] he visited the rougher taverns, like, for example, the Miriliton where he could hear Aristide Bruant sing his wicked songs;[47] he traveled extensively;[48] he was a constant spectator at the music halls, both in England and on the Continent;[49] and everywhere he went he jotted down his impressions in little notebooks.[50] Once, when invited by the *directrice* of the only *chahût* academy in the world to watch rehearsals, he went because, he said that he was always "avid of impressions and sensations," and he was particularly anxious to add some new ones to his list.[51]

Nearly all of Symons' manifold experiences find their way into his writing of this time, particularly into the poetry in which he reached perhaps the height of his creative achievement. And he recorded in his poems the minute particularities of sensation and experience with a sometimes delicate and subtle precision. For example, in "At the Cavour," from *Silhouettes*, he describes with beautiful economy the strident artificiality of the music hall and the ambiguous looks exchanged between the spectators,[52] and in the same volume records the sensations of an absinthe drinker with an exactitude which makes his previous poem about an opium smoker in *Days and Nights* seem artificial by comparison.[53]

Symons' attitude to life during these years is perhaps most effectively expressed in a poem called "Credo," which appeared in the third number of *The Yellow Book* and was afterwards reprinted as the epilogue to *London Nights*:

> Each, in himself, his hour to be and cease
> Endures alone, yet few there be who dare,
> Sole with themselves, their single burden bear,
> All the long day until the night's release.
>
> Yet, ere the night fall, and the shadows close,
> This labour of himself is each man's lot;
> All a man hath, yet living, is forgot,
> Himself he leaves behind him when he goes.
>
> If he have any valiancy within,
> If he have made his life his very own,
> If he have loved and laboured, and have known
> A strenuous virtue, and a strenuous sin;
>
> Then being dead, his life was not all vain,
> For he has saved what most desire to lose,
> And he has chosen what the few must choose,
> Since life, once lived, returns no more again.
>
> For of our time we lose so large a part
> In serious trifles, and so oft let slip
> The wine of every moment, at the lip
> Its moment, and the moment of the heart.
>
> We are awake so little on the earth,
> And we shall sleep so long, and rise so late,

If there is any knocking at that gate
Which is the gate of death, the gate of birth.[54]

From this poem it would seem that Symons had at last fallen victim to the kind of debased Epicureanism which Pater's writings appeared to sanction. But, in spite of the obvious echoes from Pater's *Renaissance* in the last two verses, one should not too hastily assume that it was Pater who had at last led Symons astray. Certainly, the conclusion to *The Renaissance* would have predisposed Symons to subscribe to the kind of conduct he describes in "Credo," but the more immediate influences on him were Huysmans and Verlaine, particularly the latter, whose life, as well as his work, would have stimulated Symons' desire to know both "strenuous virtues" and "strenuous sins."

Indeed, so keen a disciple of Verlaine did Symons become that he was one of the prime movers in a scheme to bring the Frenchman to England in 1893 to give a series of lectures on the new poetry.[55] Symons himself translated Verlaine's own account of his visit in an article in *The Savoy* which appeared three years later. Apparently Verlaine stayed with Symons in his apartment at Fountain Court, where they "talked for two good hours, about everything under the sun," and at the same time consumed "an entire box, one of those long, tall, tin boxes of tea biscuits, 'muffins in English'." Symons must have lived these moments intensely, for three years later he could still remember the details of the scene sufficiently well to observe, somewhat pedantically in a footnote, that the biscuits were "Osborne," and later, that they were washed down, not with gin and soda, as Verlaine had observed, but straight gin.[56]

At all events, the visit was a success. Verlaine's first engagement was to read some of his poetry to a group of his admirers presided over by Edmund Gosse at Barnard's Inn, where his performance impressed even Arthur Waugh, hardly a friend of the Decadents;[57] and later Verlaine gave another lecture at Oxford, presided over by Professor Frederick York-Powell, which was followed by a dinner in his honor, where again Verlaine seems to have left a pleasing impression.[58] Unfortunately, fortified with the proceeds from these two lectures, Verlaine found the gin-shops of Soho too much of a temptation and was soon penniless. However, other lectures were arranged for him in London and

Manchester, the money from which, by the arrangement of his sponsors, was paid to him in Paris.[59]

Even after Verlaine's return to Paris, Symons continued to act on his behalf, arranging for some of his poems to be printed in English reviews during Verlaine's last years, writing numerous articles about him, and translating a substantial amount of his poetry.[60] For his part, the Frenchman responded with at least three poems inspired by his visits to Oxford, Manchester, and Symons' own Fountain Court. In addition, Verlaine wrote a sympathetic review of *London Nights*, which Symons had dedicated to Verlaine, comparing his poetry to that of Byron and Tennyson, and finding in it traces of Baudelaire, Théodore de Banville, and the Parnassians.[61]

Apart from those Decadent qualities which Symons had described in his *Harper's Magazine* article, part of Verlaine's appeal for Symons was undoubtedly his bohemianism. Symons believed that an ordinary life of cleanliness and respectability did not make for good poetry. As he wrote in an early essay on Henley: "A villa and books never made a poet; they do but tend to the building up of the respectable virtues; and for the respectable virtues poetry has but the slightest use. To roam in the sun and air with vagabonds, to haunt the strange corners of cities, to know all the useless, and improper, and amusing people who are alone very much worth knowing; to live, as well as to observe life . . . it is such things as these that make for poetry." [62]

Verlaine could satisfy these requirements well enough; and, furthermore, although it was generally remarked that the Frenchman's manners and appearance were not particularly agreeable, Symons emphasizes that Verlaine, like a true Decadent, observed a gentlemanly aloofness. So, when Symons describes his initial impression of the poet, he—unlike George Moore, who had made him appear although interesting, rather sordid—gives him a more romantic appearance:

He was shabbily dressed, without a collar, a white scarf round his neck, a grey hat pushed back on his head. I had seen many portraits of him, not very nice to look at, and I had heard the most unpleasant accounts about his appearance. What I saw was something totally different. The face was a strange contradictory one, with its spiritual forehead, its animal jaw, its shifting faun's eyes. But it was quite genial, and it had a singularly manly air, I might add. The eyes were certainly curious; oblique, constantly in movement, with gestures (there is no other word) of the lids and brows.[63]

If Symons was a little generous in dealing with Verlaine's personal appearance, he did succeed in being more objective about his abilities as a poet. He recognized that there was some slovenliness in *Dédicaces*, and that this same volume was marred by an exaggerated use of some of Verlaine's technical idiosyncrasies—particularly *enjambement*—and that his control over the sonnet form was, to say the least, eccentric.[64] He regretted the appearance of *Invectives*, however, not so much for their artistic carelessness, although he does imply that there is some of this too, but rather because they distorted the image of the man by exaggerating his petulance and obscuring his essential good nature.[65]

Symons' general estimate of Verlaine is also balanced, and his observations are, on the whole, as perceptive as they are sympathetic. It is perhaps true, as Ruth Temple has pointed out, that in comparing Verlaine with Whistler, Symons does not do full justice to the "plastic" qualities of the Frenchman's work,[66] and, that he exaggerates the English influence on Verlaine's poetic manner.[67] But, certainly, in dealing with Verlaine's technique as a poetical craftsman, Symons is excellent, as is demonstrated by his early review of "Bonheur," in which he analyzes one of Verlaine's stanzas in some detail, pointing out the effect of internal rhyme, allitzeration, irregular rhythm, word repetition, and constant shifting of accent. However, even here, Symons maintained his objectivity, and, though recognizing the merit of variety, he was ready to admit that such technical virtuosity did not always make for good poetry.[68]

In spite of these reservations, Verlaine is for Symons the poet who most nearly approaches the ideal; and, in summarizing his achievement in the handling of poetic language, Symons not only provides us with an intelligent appraisal of his hero but also presents a poetic manifesto for his own poetry of this time. Verlaine, says Symons,

knows that words are living things, which we have not created, and which go their way without demanding of us the right to live. He knows that words are suspicious, not without their malice, and that they resist mere force with the implacable resistance of fire and water. They are to be caught only with guile or with trust. Verlaine has both and words become Ariel to him. . . . They transform themselves for him into music, colour and shadow; a disembodied music, diaphanous colours, luminous shadow. They serve him with so absolute a self-negation, that he can write *romances sans paroles*, songs almost without words, in which scarcely a sense of interference of human speech remains.[69]

Symons also aspired to write "songs almost without words"; and, in an effort to achieve this end, he adapted Verlaine's technical idiosyncracies to his own poetry in *Silhouettes* and *London Nights*. "Music and Memory," for example, is a poem which vividly expresses Symons' debt:

> Across the tides of music, in the night,
> Her magical face,
> A light upon it as the happy light
> Of dreams in some delicious place
> Under the moonlight in the night.
>
> Music, soft throbbing music in the night,
> Her memory swims
> Into the brain, a carol of delight;
> The cup of music overbrims
> With wine of memory, in the night.
>
> Her face across the music, in the night,
> Her face a refrain,
> A light that sings along the waves of light,
> A memory that returns again,
> Music in music, in the night.[70]

All the effects Symons had noted in the stanza from "Bonheur" are present, and even Verlaine's langorous delicacy is successfully transmuted into Symons' English. Even more remarkable, however, are Symons' direct translations from Verlaine, for not only does he translate the sense with considerable accuracy, but he also contrives to capture the poet's rhythms, which is in accordance with his belief that a translator has an obligation to render not only the poet's sense but to capture his spirit.[71] Indeed, so extraordinarily fine are some of Symons' translations from Verlaine, particularly his rendering of "Cortège" from *Fêtes Galantes*, that it is surely to be regretted that the proposed complete translation of the *Fêtes Galantes* and other poems never materialized.[72]

In other of Symons' poems of this time, although less obviously influenced by Verlaine than, say, "Music and Memory," Symons subscribes to some of the more general characteristics of Verlaine's work: the conversational tone; the selection of the trivial details of daily existence charged with a new emotional significance; and what Harold Nicolson has aptly called "the garrulous confidences of his poems." [73] These qualities that make Verlaine's poetry so personal and intimate can be recognized in Symons' poetry. And not only that, but the French poet's statement that art should be a reflection of oneself, which Symons quotes with approval in his review of "Bonheur," [74] is equally applicable to Symons' work. All this is characteristic of "White Heliotrope," one of the most typical poems in *Silhouettes:*

> The feverish room and that white bed,
> The tumbled skirts upon a chair,
> The novel flung half-open where
> Hat, hair-pins, puffs, and paints are spread;
>
> The mirror that has sucked your face
> Into its secret deep of deeps,
> And there mysteriously keeps
> Forgotten memories of grace;
>
> And you, half dressed and half awake,
> Your slant eyes strangely watching me,
> And I, who watch you drowsily,
> With eyes that, having slept not, ache;
>
> This (need one dread? nay, dare one hope?)
> Will rise, a ghost of memory, if
> Ever again my handkerchief
> Is scented with white heliotrope.[75]

As might be expected, poems such as this one earned for Symons a somewhat questionable reputation among Victorian readers. Indeed, opposition in some quarters was so strong that Symons felt called upon to justify himself; and, when the second edition of *Silhouettes* appeared in 1896, it was prefaced by a short essay setting forth his esthetic creed. He comments first on the "ingenuous reviewer" who had found his verses "unwholesome" and had taken exception to the "faint smell of Patchouli about them." But, Symons says, why not Patchouli?

Is there any 'reason in nature' why we should write exclusively about the natural blush if the delicately acquired blush of rouge has any attraction for us? Both exist: both, I think, are charming in their way: and the latter, as a subject, has, at all events, more novelty. If you prefer your 'new-mown hay' in the hayfield, and I, it may be, in a scent-bottle, why may not my individual caprice be allowed to find expression as well as yours? Probably I enjoy the hayfield as much as you do: but I enjoy quite other scents and sensations as well, and I take the former for granted, and write my poem, for a change, about the latter. There is no necessary difference in artistic value between a good poem about a flower in the hedge and a good poem about the scent in a sachet.

Then he continues, somewhat defensively:

I do not wish to assert that the kind of verse which happened to reflect certain moods at a certain period of my life, is the best kind of verse in itself, or is likely to seem to me, in other years, when other moods may have made them their own, the best kind of verse for my own expression of myself. Nor do I affect to doubt that the creation of the supreme emotion is a higher form of art than the reflection of the most exquisite sensation, the evocation of the most magical impression. I claim only an equal liberty for the rendering of every mood of that variable and inexplicable and contradictory creature which we call ourselves, of every aspect under which we are gifted or condemned to apprehend the beauty and strangeness and curiosity of the visible world.[76]

III The Savoy

Symons made a somewhat similar pronouncement in the first number of *The Savoy,* a journal which he edited and which was, in a sense, an offshoot of the perhaps better known *Yellow Book.* The fifth issue of *The Yellow Book* had appeared in April, 1895, which was also the time of the Oscar Wilde trial; and, although Wilde had never written anything for the journal nor was particularly well acquainted with any of its contributors, it was generally assumed that he and *The Yellow Book* were intimately associated. So it was that the periodical itself came under fire, and Aubrey Beardsley, one of its main illustrators, whose pen-and-ink portraits of perverse, sin-wasted creatures had aroused considerable controversy from the beginning, was forced to resign.[77] Thereafter, editorial policy was not to favor work of a Decadent tinge, the magazine became almost respectable, and its quality declined.

However, in an effort to provide a periodical which would carry on the traditions of the early numbers of *The Yellow Book,* it was decided that a new publication should be launched, and in January, 1896, the first number of *The Savoy* appeared. The idea for the new magazine was conceived in Dieppe, where Beardsley and Symons had fled after Wilde's disgrace, not because they were in any way connected with the scandal, but simply because it was sufficient to have been distantly associated with Wilde to incur public censure.[78] Apparently, Leonard Smithers, a publisher of some notoriety who had a reputation for being a purveyor of erotica, approached Symons with plans for a new magazine. Symons consented, naming Beardsley as his art editor. Originally, it was intended that the magazine should appear quarterly; but, with the third issue, it became a monthly, a change of policy which Symons later regretted.[79]

In the first issue Symons stated his policy; he hoped to "appeal to the tastes of the intelligent by not being original for originality's sake, or audacious for the sake of advertisement, or timid for the convenience of the elderly-minded. We intend to print no verse which has not some close relationship with poetry, no fiction which has not a certain sense of what is finest in living fact, no criticism which has not some knowledge, discernment, and sincerity in its judgment." [80]

With this ideal in mind he sought among the younger group of writers for work which seemed to him most personal and noteworthy, and, as he said, he chose deliberately "from as many schools as possible to make the magazine truly representative of the literature of the period." [81] Consequently, although the general tone was more clearly Decadent than that of the early numbers of *The Yellow Book,* literary contributions from W. B. Yeats, Joseph Conrad, and George Bernard Shaw helped to give *The Savoy* a more healthy appearance. Similarly, although Beardsley left his stamp most heavily on the art of the magazine, contributions from such people as Phil May, Joseph Pennell, and William Rothenstein tended to offset the effect Beardsley must have made.

On the whole, the first issue contained little that could have offended the English reading public of the time, and it was fairly well received. Although *Punch* was heavily satiric in suggesting that *The Savoy* "should be on every school room table, every mother should present it to her daughter, for it is bound to have an ennobling and purifying influence," [82] *The Academy* maintained that "the commonplaces of literary pessimism and the easy ingenuities of an unsavoury subject (upon which reputations of a moment have been built, as upon sand) are alike absent from *The Savoy*." [83] Even *The Athenaeum* grudgingly admitted that, although it was apparently "an offshoot of *The Yellow Book*, and although many of the contributors are the same, it is free from some of the offences of the older periodical." [84]

Other voices, however, were not so eager to praise it. T. W. Rolleston and George Russell (AE), two of Yeats's friends, cautioned the Irish poet against having anything to do with such a disreputable publication. Russell, who was particularly strong in his denunciation, called *The Savoy* "the organ of the incubi and the succubi" and declared that "it is all mud from a muddy spring, any pure thought that mingles must lose its purity." [85] Yeats, who was also aware of the general tenor of *The Savoy*, later declared that, if an excuse for the magazine's more characteristically Decadent pieces could have been put forward, it would have been that literature demanded an explanation of all aspects of human experience. He himself seems to have associated with the magazine and to have condoned its aims "out of sheer mischief, of sheer delight in the play of the mind." [86]

On the whole, the public accepted *The Savoy* fairly gracefully; and it is ironic that Yeats's own articles on Blake, not written certainly "out of sheer mischief," were mainly responsible for antagonizing public opinion. In volumes three, four, and five these articles appeared, together with reproductions of Blake's illustration of *The Divine Comedy*. One of these reproductions, "Antaeus Setting Virgil and Dante Upon the Verge of Cocytus," so displeased one of the leading booksellers, W. H. Smith and Sons, who were responsible for circulating a large number of copies of *The Savoy* through their newsstands at railway stands and elsewhere, that they refused to carry it any longer, and immediately the magazine's financial position became grave.[87] Indeed, its finances became so straitened that, when *The Savoy* appeared for the last time, it was written entirely by the editor himself.

Throughout its short life *The Savoy* published a great deal of Symons' work, most of it decidedly Decadent in tone, and in keeping with the Decadent formulas described in his *Harper's Magazine* article of 1893. The essay "At the Alhambra" is typical. Subtitled "Impressions and Sensations," Symons writes of the fleeting impression he once received when, passing outside the theater, he caught a glimpse through an open door of a ballet being performed inside: "In the general way I prefer to see my illusions very clearly, recognising them as illusions, and yet, to my own perverse and decadent way of thinking, losing none of their charm." [88] He finds the "frank artificiality" of the dancers' "painted faces" and "tawdry ornaments . . . exquisite"; and he offers an additional refinement of the perverse when, commenting on the dancers at rehearsal and devoid of their finery and makeup, he declares that "in this fantastic return to nature I found the last charm of the artificial." [89]

Although the contents of *The Savoy* were of a genuinely high standard, perhaps the magazine's most notable achievement was the way it drew together the literary and artistic life of London and Paris, a union of cultures which was to increase in importance in the early years of the twentieth century and which was to influence the development of the modern esthetic. As Thomas Jay Garbaty has pointed out, the idea to publish such a journal as *The Savoy* was conceived in Dieppe; the magazine devoted a great deal of its space to popularizing contemporary French literature; even the English contributions were either written in France or reflected interest in French life; the French press, notably the *Courier*, gave it favorable reviews;[90] and, one might add, it even inspired a short-lived French journal called *Le Centaur*.[91] In short, *The Savoy* was an Anglo-French periodical, the first of its kind; and therefore it is something of a landmark in the history of English literature.

IV *Rejection of the Decadent Creed*

Symons' excursion to Paris in 1889 and those which quickly followed exerted a profound effect upon both his life and his art. They provided him with an opportunity to clarify and formulate his intentions as a writer, and in Verlaine he found a model whose poetic technique he could follow to good advantage. It is true that a desire to imitate all things French was in the air. It is also true that many who sought their inspiration across the Channel were prompted by the feeling in certain literary circles that it was the right thing to do; and one cannot deny that, in many literary productions of the time, Gaul is somewhat factitiously introduced.

But, in spite of what some critics may say, Symons' connections with France were far from superficial. Richard le Gallienne, for example, obviously had Symons in mind when in his arrogant, versified preface to *English Poems* he adjured his contemporaries to seek inspiration at home rather than across the Channel.[92] In his review of Symons' *Silhouettes*, Le Gallienne was yet more specific in acknowledging his distaste for the contemporary adoration of France, finding Symons' yearning for Paris rather pathetic, in so far as it reflected the traditional, romantic longing of the provincial for the sophisticated world.[93] Perhaps there was something "provincial" in Symons' fondness for France, but the eagerness with which he plunged into Left Bank bohemianism and his enthusiasm for all things Parisian suggest that there was something more.

Symons himself has given some indication as to what this attraction was, for in an autobiographical chapter which appeared in a later collection of essays, he recalls: "If I have been a vagabond, and have never been able to root myself in any one place in the world, it is because I have no early memories of any one sky or soil. It has freed me from many prejudices in giving me its own unresting kind of freedom; but it has cut me out from whatever is stable, of long growth in the world." [94] It is hardly surprising, then, that the bohemian, cosmopolitan "rootless" life among the cafés of the Left Bank in the 1890's should have exercised such a strong fascination for him.

However, one should remember that this confession was made by Symons in his maturity; and there is in his remarks a certain wistfulness, a regret, that such has been his fortune. At first, however, if the poems of *Silhouettes* are any indication, he regarded this restlessness as more of a blessing than otherwise. He exults in his freedom and glories in the fact that he can "love" for experience alone. He is drawn to women whose synthetic charms seem to offer the prospect of an unconventional liaison, as for example, in the poem "Maquillage," where "the charm of rouge on fragile cheeks" suggests to him the possibilities of "perfumed hours of day, and doubtful night/Of alcoves curtained close against the light." [95]

Symons always tries to avoid becoming too deeply involved, for this can only bring unhappiness. Far better it is "to be loved and to love for a little, and then/Well, to forget, be forgotten, ere loving grow life!",[96] even though this is sometimes impossible. Once, the poet recalls:

> Our love was all arrayed in pleasantness,
> A tender little love that sighed and smiled
> At little happy nothings, like a child,
> A dainty little love in fancy dress.
>
> But now the love that once was half in play
> Has come to be this grave and piteous thing.
> Why did you leave me all the suffering
> For all your memory when you went away?
>
> You might have played the play out, O my friend,
> Closing upon a kiss our comedy.
> Or is it, then, a fault of taste in me,
> Who like no tragic exit at the end? [97]

In this poem the poet can treat his misfortune ironically; but, as he becomes more conscious of the disillusionment that is the likely end of such liaisons, his bitterness increases. As a result, in the next volume of poems, *London Nights*, the first two pieces express with some violence his dissatisfaction with what seems to be the inevitability of disillusionment:

> My life is like a music-hall,
> Where, in the impotence of rage,
> Chained by enchantment to my stall,
> I see myself upon the stage
> Dance to amuse a music-hall.
>
> 'Tis I that smoke this cigarette,
> Lounge here, and laugh for vacancy
> And watch the dancers turn; and yet
> It is my very self I see
> Across the cloudy cigarette.

My very self that turns and trips,
Painted, pathetically gay,
An empty song upon the lips
In make-believe of holiday:
I, I, this thing that turns and trips!

The light flares in the music-hall,
The light, the sound, that weary us;
Hour follows hour, I count them all,
Lagging, and loud, and riotous;
My life is like a music-hall.[98]

Then, in Symons' next volume of poems, *Amoris Victima,* which appeared in 1897, an even stronger statement of the poet's dissatisfaction appears, in "Moonrise," [99] and in the very last poem of the collection, "Mundi Victima," Symons speaks in the spirit of total disillusionment:

Benignant principalities and powers
Of evil, powers of the world's abysmal hours,
Take me and make me yours: I am yours: O take
The sacrifice of soul and body, break
The mould of this void spirit, scatter it
Into the vague and shoreless infinite,
Pour it upon the restless arrogant
Winds of tumultuous spaces; grant, O grant
That the loosed sails of this determinate soul
Hurry it to disaster, and the goal
Of swiftest shipwreck; that this soul descend
The unending depths until oblivion end
In self-oblivion, and at last be lost
Where never any other wandering ghost,
Voyaging from other worlds remembered not,
May find it and remind it of things forgot.[100]

Paul Elmer More has called the poems in these volumes "a tragic history," [101] but William Archer found them "insistently monotonous." [102] Although most modern readers would be inclined to agree with Archer rather than with More, there is some justification for the more sympathetic view. In spite of the irritating self-consciousness, a Byronic self-dramatization which becomes increasingly tiresome, these poems do seem to have been inspired by a deeply felt, personal emotion. This interpretation is clearly supported by Symons himself in an article he published in a notorious little magazine which appeared in the 1920's called *The Two Worlds;* in it he explicitly states that the poems he wrote during these years were firmly rooted in his personal experience.[103]

Perhaps even more dramatic evidence is provided from among the unpublished documents in the Symons Collection at Princeton, and in particular in a little pamphlet which was printed privately by Symons in 1940, *Amoris Victima.* From these documents it is clear that Symons, during the early years of the 1890's, entered into a series of affairs with various women, mostly actresses and dancers, all of whom he seems to have been able to treat with ironic disdain and true Decadent detachment. However, in 1893 or 1894 Symons met "Lydia," the "Bianca" of a number of poems in *London Nights,* and the personage who lies behind nearly all the poems in the 1897 collection *Amoris Victima.* Lydia—supposedly the illegitimate daughter of a Spanish gypsy and an English woman—was a dancer at the Empire, beautiful, and, if one is to believe Symons, a curious mixture of saintliness and perversity: in short, Lydia was admirably cast for the role of the enigmatic *femme fatale.* For Symons, his love for her became an obsession; and, although she returned his affection, it was evidently a tempestuous courtship which resulted in Symons alternately "escaping" from her ambiguous charms to take refuge in his work on the Continent and agonizing over her in an ecstacy of frustrated sexuality. Finally, she married someone else and eventually passed out of his life, but not from his memory, as poem after poem written by Symons in his declining years testifies.[104]

Such, no doubt, was the immediate cause of Symons' increasing *accidia,* but there were other elements in his life at this time which must have contributed to his growing depression. In March, 1896, Symons' mother died; and, although—judging by his remarks about her in the autobiographical first chapter of *Spiritual Adventures*—he seems not to have been strongly attached to her, it is clear he felt for her considerable affection.[105] Almost three years before her death he had addressed a sonnet to her, which certainly suggests both compassion and respect,[106] and it is also worth noting that her name was Lydia. The coincidental loss of two Lydias in such a short space of time must have made a deep impression on him, for Symons was ever susceptible to superstitious fears. At the root of his depression, however, was perhaps, the fact that "the unresting kind of freedom" which Symons experienced was not such a blessing after all; he might have found greater peace if he had not been cut off "from whatever is stable, of long growth in the world." As it was, Symons felt terror; and the only relief from it is what Paul Elmer More has called "the repose of utter oblivion and the escape from self in perfect death." However, Symons had not reached "the point of no return." He had pursued the Decadent ideal to a point similar to that which des Esseintes had reached at the end of *A Rebours*, and what was left for him was the muzzle of the pistol or the foot of the cross. But Symons was not a conventionally religious man, and the Catholic Church was not to claim him as it did so many of his contemporaries, including his beloved Verlaine, whom Symons believed was also converted as a result of his having explored all the possibilities life has to offer.[107] Instead, Symons fell under the influence of W. B. Yeats, who introduced him to his own version of the spirit world; and, although Symons was not to become a particularly faithful disciple, he did find a new philosophy which was to provide him with at least temporary solace and, incidentally, provide him with the basis for a new esthetic.

CHAPTER 3

Arthur Symons: Symbolist: 1

W. B. YEATS had been predisposed to mysticism from his earliest years. Although his father, John Butler Yeats, a thorough skeptic, had done his best to persuade William to what he considered was the only really valid point of view, his efforts had met with little success. Even during his adolescence, William was more than a little doubtful of the adequacy of the rationalist's position; and, after he had become close friends with George Russell, whose faith in the spirit world was as unshakeable as Yeats's father's belief in its non-existence, William became even more convinced that a purely rational view of the universe had its limitations.[1]

I Symons and Yeats

So, in 1885, Yeats and Russell gathered about them a group of young people dissatisfied with their religion but avid for mystery, and formed The Dublin Hermetic Society, dedicated to the study of European magic, mysticism, and Eastern religion. Two years later the Yeats family moved to London, but William continued his occult studies with the Theosophists under Mme. Blavatsky, a lady whose integrity had previously been impugned by Richard Hodgson in 1885. After being with the Theosophists for only a short while, Yeats, too, began to entertain suspicions about the potency of Mme. Blavatsky's control over the supernatural, openly proclaimed his skepticism, and was abruptly excommunicated.[2] However, charlatan or not, Mme. Blavatsky reinforced Yeats's opinion that the spirit world did exist; and he was encouraged to investigate further. Accordingly, even before he had been expelled from the Theosophists, Yeats had become interested in another occult society, The Hermetic Society of the Golden

Dawn, similarly dedicated to research in the supernatural; and he pursued his studies there.[3]

Also, between 1889 and 1893, Yeats collaborated with his father's friend, Edwin Ellis, to bring out the *Collected Works of William Blake* and to publish a long essay which attempted to unravel the complexities of Blake's writings. Although, as Yeats himself relates, his mind "had been full of Blake from boyhood up," [4] he was led to look at him more closely at this time because of his evident similarities with the occultists he had been studying.[5]

At this time, when Yeats was most diligently exploring the possibilities of the spirit world, he first met Symons. The exact date of their first meeting is not known, but Yeats first mentions him in a letter dated March, 1891, to Katherine Tynan. He refers to a recent poem of his own, "A Man Who Dreamed of Fairyland," which had just appeared in the *National Observer,* asks her whether she had liked it, and adds: "Henley liked it very much and some friends here say it is my best; that is to say Arthur Symons and Edward Garnett do." [6] Also about this time, Yeats, together with Ernest Rhys and T. W. Rolleston, founded the Rhymers' Club, which they hoped would attract the leading poets of the day and afford them an opportunity to read and discuss their work with fellow members. Meetings were held in an upstairs room of the Cheshire Cheese in Fleet Street, London, and thither went such writers as Ernest Dowson, Richard Le Gallienne, Herbert Horne, Lionel Johnson, John Todhunter, John Davidson, Victor Plarr and, of course, Arthur Symons; so it seems likely that Yeats met Symons there.

At first Yeats seems to have been drawn more towards Lionel Johnson, but when Johnson's alcoholism became noticeably excessive and when his impressive anecdotes of the famous people he had met grew more and more obviously fictitious, Yeats cooled and became more intimate with Symons.[7] Yeats's first impressions of Symons were not, however, very flattering; and he tells us that at first he was "repelled by Symons because with a superficial deduction I suppose from the chapter in Marius, 'Anima Vagula'— Marius was I think our contemporary classic, he saw nothing in literature but a source of impassioned philosophy." [8] Nevertheless, Yeats did admire Symons' poetic technique. Lionel Johnson

might sneer at Symons' "Parisian impressionism," [9] but Yeats felt
that Symons, together with Horne, Dowson, and Johnson himself,
did have something which he lacked: "conscious deliberate craft,
and what I must always lack, scholarship." [10]

Furthermore, Symons and his fellow Rhymers were devoted to
their craft, almost to the exclusion of everything else, and, in ret-
rospect, Yeats could say that these writers taught him the value of
restraint and the value of developing a technique "sufficiently flex-
ible for expression of the emotions of life as they arise." [11]

Yeats became more interested in Symons, however, when he
discovered that, unlike the other members of the club, he did
seem to regard poetry as a vital force, as an art which invited
theoretical speculation. Such an attitude, however, did not appeal
to the other Rhymers. In a newspaper article of 1892, Yeats mentions the irritation he himself provoked when he attempted "to
explain a philosophy of poetry which showed the dependence, as
I conceived it, of all great art and literature upon conviction and
upon heroic life." [12] And Symons fared no better; he would sometimes say: "We are concerned with nothing but 'impressions', but
that itself was a generalisation and met with a stony silence." [13]
The trouble was, that to the Rhymers ". . . literature had ceased
to be the handmaid of humanity, and become instead a terrible
queen, in whose service the stars rose and set, and for whose
pleasure life stumbles along in the darkness." [14]

But for Symons, as for Yeats, poetry was a useful art; and, just
because it was useful, it deserved to be talked about and examined closely in an effort to establish dogmas which might clarify
its function and make apparent its usefulness. Consequently,
Yeats found that he did have something in common with Symons.
They visited Paris together in 1894, where Symons introduced him
to Verlaine, and took him to see Villiers de l'Isle Adam's *Axel,*
where Symons supplemented Yeats's imperfect understanding of
the French language with paraphrases and comments, sufficient to
enable him to write a review of the play for *The Bookman.*[15]
Shortly after they returned to England, Yeats took rooms next to
Symons' in Fountain Court, and thereafter the two poets enjoyed
an increasing familiarity.[16]

Symons was apparently a good man to talk with, and Yeats tells
us that he had a facility for slipping "as it were into the mind of
another" and that his own "thoughts gained in richness and clear-

ness from his sympathy." Yeats also wondered just how much of his own theory and practice he owed to passages that Symons read to him from Catullus, Verlaine, and Mallarmé, and, on looking back, it seemed to him that he and Symons

. . . always discussed life at its most intense moment, that moment which gives a common sacredness to the Song of Songs, and to the Sermon on the Mount, and in which one discovers something supernatural, a stirring as it were, of the roots of the hair. He was making those translations from Mallarmé and from Verlaine, from Calderon, from St. John of the Cross, which are the most accomplished metrical translations of our time, and I think that those from Mallarmé may have given elaborate form to my verses of those years, to the later poems of *The Wind Among the Reeds*, to *The Shadowy Waters*, while Villiers de l'Isle Adam had shaped whatever in my *Rosa Alchemica* Pater had not shaped.[17]

Once, too, after reading Tolstoy's *Anna Karenina*, Yeats considered whether ". . . an individual with great emotional intensity might follow the pilgrims as it were to some unknown shrine, and give to all those separated elements and to all that abstract love and melancholy, a symbolical, a mythological coherence. Not Chaucer's rough-tongued riders, but rather an ended pilgrimage, a procession of the Gods! Arthur Symons brought back from Paris stories of Verhaeren and Maeterlinck, and so brought me confirmation, as I thought, and I began to announce a poetry like that of the Sufi's." [18]

At first, it seems curious that Symons was responsible for suggesting the possibilities of mystical poetry, for his own work up to this time, both in prose and poetry, would hardly seem to indicate interests in this direction. Furthermore, Symons' temperament, as Yeats describes it, seems not at all the kind to interest itself in this type of poetry. Yeats describes their first visit to Paris together, when Symons treated him "with a now admiring, now mocking wonder, because being in love, and in no way lucky in that love [with Maud Gonne]" he had grown "exceedingly puritanical" as far as his "immediate neighbourhood was concerned."

On the other hand, Symons' approach to life was quite different. One night, Yeats recalls, when they were strolling near the Luxembourg, "a strange young woman in bicycling costume, came out of a sidestreet, threw one arm around [Symons'] neck, walked beside us in perfect silence for a hundred yards or so, and then darted up another sidestreet." Evidently Yeats was not amused; for, later that evening when they were sitting in a café, he looked up from his English newspaper to find himself surrounded by "painted ladies." He angrily referred them to Symons, saying, "That gentleman over there, has never refused wine or coffee to a lady," and soon they were all "settled about him like greedy pigeons."

In attempting to account for Symons' behavior, Yeats concluded that he was not interested in "passion," and then continued: "A woman drew him to her by some romantic singularity in her beauty or her circumstance, and drew him the more if the curiosity she aroused were half intellectual. A little after the time I write of, throwing himself into my chair after some visit to a music-hall or hippodrome, he began, 'O, Yeats, I was never in love with a serpent-charmer before'. He was objective. For him 'the visible world existed', as he was fond of quoting, and I suspect him of a Moon that had entered its fourth quarter." [19] Such a person seems hardly suited for the role of a mystical go-between, and it is indeed doubtful that Symons was able to lay before Yeats an explicit theory which would convince him that his contemporaries in France would serve as effective models for one who would write poetry "like that of the Sufi's."

What seems to have happened is that Yeats, preoccupied with supernaturalism and anxious to find a suitable vehicle for its expression, gradually became aware that those writers whom Symons had previously labeled "Decadent," might have greater mystical potentiality than Symons realized. Blake was, as Yeats implied later, not an altogether satisfactory model; his symbology was too personal and, more important, too inflexible for the needs of a poet wishing to express his own vision. Furthermore, "a systematic mystic," such as Blake, is not the greatest kind of artist because "his imagination is too great to be bounded by a picture or a song, and because only imperfection in a mirror of perfection, or perfection in a mirror of imperfection delights our frailty." Far more satisfactory would be a "fragmentary symbolist" because, "while he evokes in his persons and his landscapes an infinite emotion, a perfected emotion, a part of the Divine Essence, he does not set his symbols in the great procession as Blake would have him, 'in a certain order suited' to his 'imaginative energy'." [20]

In "The Decadent Movement in Literature" had not Symons stressed the "perfection" of the Decadents in fixing the last fine shade, and had he not, in writing of Verlaine at least, pointed to the intensity of feeling and emotion which he had packed into the impression? Might it not be possible then, to conceive of these moments as the point where communication with the "Divine Essence" becomes possible? So it was that in their conversations Yeats and Symons always reverted to discussion of life and art at its most intense moment; and it seems likely that these talks prompted Symons to look again at his Decadent writers from a different point of view and to see them at last not simply as artistic perfectionists, whose primary concern was to explore abnormal behavior and spotlight the fleeting "impression," but as writers who sought transcendence through their art.

II   The Symbolist Movement in Literature

The results of this reassessment appeared in what is probably Symons' best known and most important work, *The Symbolist Movement in Literature*.[21] Like all books, it is not uniformly good throughout; and its general organization was not improved by Symons' subsequent revisions.[22] But what is most remarkable, perhaps, is that the author of "The Decadent Movement in Literature," a poet who had won a name for himself as a "fleshly" poet, should have sufficiently changed his outlook to write sympathetically about the mystical elements in the work of writers in which, only a few years ago, he had found primarily "an intense self-consciousness, a restless curiosity in research, a spiritual and moral perversity."

The events which led up to this surprising *volte face* were almost certainly personal; for, as it has been noted, 1895–1896 was for Symons a time of crisis; and his present interest in matters mystical was probably occasioned by his recognition of the dangers implicit in the hedonist's creed. It is even possible to be fairly precise in dating Symons' change of attitude, for spiritual enlightenment seems to have come to him while vacationing with Yeats in Ireland during the summer of 1896. In February, Symons, still in London, had written the preface to the second edition of *Silhouettes*, in which he defended his poems against certain critics who had found them "unwholesome" because of their "faint smell of Patchouli." Later that year, in September, when Symons and

Yeats were together in Sligo, Symons wrote his preface to the second edition of *London Nights;* and, although he again feels constrained to defend himself against the "singular unanimity of abuse" that his volume of poems had called forth, his argument is slightly, but significantly, different.

The poems in this volume have been called "immoral," but, says Symons, art and morals are two quite different things:

Is it for such a shifting guide that I am to forsake the sure and constant leading of art, which tells me that whatever I find in humanity (passion, desire, the spirit of the senses, the hell or heaven of man's heart) is part of the eternal substance which nature weaves in the rough for art to combine cunningly into beautiful patterns? The whole visible world itself, we are told, is but a symbol, made visible in order that we may apprehend ourselves, and not be blown hither and thither like a flame in the night. How laughable it is, then, that we should busy ourselves, with such serious faces, in the commending or condemning, the permission or the exemption, of this accident or that, this or the other passing caprice of our wisdom or our folly, as a due or improper subject for the 'moment's monument' of a poem.[23]

Symons now minimizes the importance of outward circumstance and adopts an attitude similar to that of Yeats in stressing the superior significance of an extra-sensory state in which the niceties of human behavior are unimportant. Earlier in the preface, Symons also easily calls upon a quotation from Blake to support a minor point in his argument[24] and, most interestingly of all, instead of using the word "impressions" he adopts the more Yeatsian "moods." And he employs it, as he had not in the previous preface, with something approaching the meaning which Yeats habitually gave it:

The moods of men! There I find my subject, there the region over which art rules: and whatever has once been a mood of mine, though it has been no more than a ripple on the sea, and had no longer than that ripple's duration, I claim the right to render, if I can, in verse: and I claim, from my critics and my readers, the primary understanding, that a mood is after all but a mood, a ripple on the sea, and perhaps no longer than that ripple's duration. I do not profess that any poem in this book is the record of actual fact: I declare that every poem is the sincere attempt to render a particular mood which has once been mine, and to render it as if, for the moment, there were no other mood for me in the world. I have rendered, well or ill, many moods, and without disguise or preference. If it be objected to me that some of them were moods I had better never have felt, I am ready to answer, Possibly: but I must add, What of that? They have existed: and whatever has existed has achieved the right of artistic existence.[25]

A more specific instance of Yeats's influence on Symons, or to be more exact, Ireland's, is mentioned in the sixth issue of *The Savoy* in an essay entitled "From a Castle in Ireland," which also dates from the time the two men were vacationing together. The major part of the essay is simply descriptive, but Symons concludes with these words:

Among these solid and shifting things, in this castle which is at once so ancient a reality and so essential a dream, I feel myself to be in some danger of loosening the tightness of my hold upon external things, of foregoing many delectable pleasures, of forgetting many things that I have passionately learnt in cities. If I lived here too long I should forget that I am a Londoner and remember I am a Cornishman. And that would so sadly embarrass my good friends of the Celtic Renaissance! No, decidedly I have no point among those remote idealists: I must come back to London; for I have perceived the insidious danger of idealism ever since I came into these ascetic regions.[26]

That Symons' vacation in Ireland with Yeats endangered his hold on the actual is not in doubt; for, under Yeats's tutelage, Symons began to see visions. While they were staying with Edward Martyn at Tillyra Castle, his permanent residence, Yeats invoked the moon and was rewarded with the sight of "a galloping centaur, and a moment later a naked woman of incredible beauty, standing upon a pedestal and shooting an arrow at a star." The next morning Symons spoke to Yeats concerning a visionary incident of the night before—a dream he had had involving a beautiful (but clothed) woman who did not, however, carry a bow and arrow, and to whom he had composed a scrap of verse,[27] a poem which he eventually published in *Love's Cruelty*, some twenty-five years later.[28] Shortly after his visionary experience Symons went to stay with George Pollexfen, Yeats's uncle; and two years later, in March, 1898, Symons received from him his horoscope, which he kept by him until his death.[29]

III *Symbolism Redefined*

There is little doubt, therefore, that the summer of 1896 was the time of Symons' conversion; and, in the Introduction to *The Symbolist Movement in Literature*, he makes explicit acknowledgment to Yeats as the man who was immediately responsible for his spiritual enlightenment. In the first place, he dedicates the book to his friend, "both as an expression of a deep personal friendship" and because Yeats, the chief representative of the Symbolist movement in England, will be sympathetic to what he has to say. Then he continues:

I speak often in this book of Mysticism, and that I, of all people, should venture to speak, not quite as an outsider, of such things, will probably be a surprise to many. It will be no surprise to you, for you have seen me gradually finding my way, uncertainly, but inevitably, in that direction which has always been to you your natural direction. Still, as I am so meshed about with the variable world and the too clinging appearance of things, so weak before the delightfulness of earthly circumstance, I hesitate sometimes in saying what I have in mind, lest I should seem to be saying more that I have a right to say.[30]

Nevertheless, Symons did speak out, and what he had to say shows how thoroughly he subscribed to his newly found mystical creed. Previously, in "The Decadent Movement in Literature," Symons had chosen to label the whole movement as Decadent, and he had seen Symbolism as only a part of it. He now reverses the emphasis, insisting that the movement itself is Symbolist, and Decadence was merely a "mock interlude," which diverted the attention of writers while something more serious was in preparation. Furthermore, Symons now makes clear that the word "Decadent" should be applied only to style: "to that ingenious deformation of the language in Mallarmé, for instance, which can be compared with what we are accustomed to call the Greek and Latin of the Decadence." The main impetus behind the movement, as he now sees it, "is all an attempt to spiritualize literature." So he looks to the future, conscious of the heavy responsibility that poetry has taken on, "for in speaking to us so intimately, so solemnly, as only religion had hitherto spoken to us, it becomes itself a kind of religion, with all the duties and responsibilities of the sacred ritual."[31]

Yeats, of course, had said something similar in "The Autumn of the Body," an essay evidently inspired by what Symons had said elsewhere about the Symbolist writers of France. Yeats recalls how in his early poetry "he had wished to describe outward things as vividly as possible," and how he had then moved on to a delight in the "spiritual and unemphatic." Possibly with Symons in mind, he then says that "man has wooed and won the world, and has fallen weary" and that now he "must be philosophical above everything, even about the arts, for he can only return the way he came, and so escape weariness, by philosophy."

Finally, in language that clearly foreshadows Symons' remarks on the "responsibility" of poetry, Yeats states: "The Arts are, I believe, about to take upon their shoulders the burdens that have fallen from the shoulders of priests, and to lead us back upon our journey by filling our thoughts with the essence of things." Thus the poetry of the future will be "a poetry of essences, separated one from another in little and intense poems," and the result of "an ever more arduous search for an almost disembodied ecstasy." [32]

However, if Yeats had been disposed to agree with Symons' ideas on the responsibilities of poetry, he did not fully appreciate what Symons had written in *The Symbolist Movement*. As he confided to Lady Gregory on March 29, 1900, he found the work "curiously vague in its philosophy," and he felt that Symons had not really thought through the problems involved. He did concede, however, that the book contained "a great deal of really fine criticism." [33] What might have upset Yeats was Symons' failure to be particularly precise in his definition of the spirit world or even of the word "symbol."

In the essay on Gérard de Nerval, for instance, Symons seems to regard the spirit world as an ideal state which all but contradicts the world of appearance.[34] On the other hand, Mallarmé's symbols, Symons implies, suggest a reality just beyond our normal perceptions, for he attempts "to find a new, an older, sense in the so worn-out forms of things," [35] and similarly Maeterlinck searches for "the secret of things which is just beyond the most subtle words." [36] For Verlaine, the spirit world can be apprehended through the circumstances of this world when viewed with some intensity;[37] and Rimbaud too—who lived with all his faculties all the time, who pursued the "absolute," and who was forced to give up writing because "he could be content with nothing less"—evidently conceived of the spirit world in a similar way.[38] With Villiers de l'Isle Adam, even more than with Nerval, this state was "against the evidence of the senses, against the negations of materialistic science, against the monstrous paradox of progress, against his own pessimism in the fact of these formidable enemies," [39] but Huysmans found the absolute in apprehending the organic unity of the universe.[40]

Such inconsistency in Symons' attitude to the spirit world and the means by which it may be apprehended is certainly annoying, and Richard Ellmann is surely right in suggesting that it constitutes a major defect in the book as a whole.[41] But Symons was not searching for a consistent philosophy; he merely sought intimations of spirituality, earthly manifestations of a world which lay beyond the senses. And this intent is clear from the conclusion in which he tells, first, that man's only chance for complete happiness in this world is by "shutting the eyes of the mind, and deadening its sense of learning, and dulling the keenness of its apprehension of the unknown."

But, second, he suggests there is something ignoble in this kind of escape, for "only very young people want to be happy. What we all want is to be quite sure that there is something which makes it worthwhile to go on living, in what seems to us our best way, at our finest intensity; something beyond the mere fact that we are satisfying a sort of inner logic (which may be quite faulty) and that we get our best makeshift for happiness on that so hazardous assumption."

Hence, he says, arises the importance of mysticism, "with which all this symbolical literature has so much to do," which presents us "not with a guide for conduct, not with a plan for our happiness, not with an explanation of any mystery, but with a theory of life which makes us familiar with mystery, and which seems to harmonise those instincts which make for religion, passion and art, freeing us at once of a great bondage. The final uncertainty remains, but we seem to knock less helplessly at closed doors, coming so much closer to the once terrifying eternity of things about us, as we come to look upon these things as shadows, through which we have our own shadowy passage." And it is impossible not to catch the personal note in the following:

As we realise the identity of a poem, a prayer, or a kiss, in that spiritual universe which we are weaving for ourselves, each out of a thread of the great fabric; as we realise the infinite insignificance of action, its immense distance from the current of life; as we realise the delight of feeling ourselves carried onward by forces which it is our wisdom to obey; it is at least with a certain relief that we turn to an ancient doctrine, so much the more likely to be true because it has so much the air of a dream. On this theory alone does all life become worth living, all art worth making, all worship worth offering.[42]

Exhausted by a life dedicated to the gratification of the senses, Symons sought transcendence; and the surest way to heaven was up a Symbolist Parnassus. Like Arnold, only in a different way and for different reasons, Symons had come to find in literature a surrogate for religion.

But Yeats, unlike Symons, seems to have regarded Symbolist literature primarily as a potential model for the poetry he wished to write. Previous to his association with Symons, Yeats's poetry had been somewhat restricted in its scope. His knowledge of Irish folklore and myth and his study of Blake and Mme. Blavatsky had given him a useful symbology which enabled him to extend the spiritual dimensions of his poetry; but, even so, it lacked universality: Irish symbols were too local, and Rosicrucian ones too esoteric. Hence Yeats's initial enthusiasm for the French Symbolists, and particularly for Mallarmé, whose precise but widely evocative symbolism seemed to provide an effective solution. As Yeats wrote in "Symbolism in Poetry," the poetry of the future would involve the "casting out of descriptions of nature for the sake of nature, of the moral law for the sake of the moral law, a casting out of all anecdotes and . . . brooding over scientific opinion . . . , and of that vehemence that would make us do certain things. . . ." Also,

with this change of substance, this return to imagination, this understanding that the laws of art, which are the hidden laws of the world, can alone bind the imagination, would come a change of style, and we would cast out of serious poetry those energetic rhythms, as of a man running . . . , and we would seek out those wavering meditative, organic rhythms, which are the embodiment of the imagination, that neither desires nor hates, because it has done with time, and only

LIBRARY

WAYNE STATE COLLEGE

WAYNE, NEBRASKA

wishes to gaze upon some reality, some beauty; nor would it be any
longer possible for anybody to deny the importance of form, in all its
kinds, for although you can expound an opinion, or describe a thing,
when your words are not quite well chosen, you cannot give body to
something that moves beyond the senses, unless your words are as
subtle, as complex, as full of voluptuous life, as the body of a flower
or of a woman.[43]

This is fine rhetoric, but it is doubtful whether Yeats fully understood the implications of the kind of poetry he aspired to write
or, indeed, was fully aware of the complexities of symbolism. For
example, in his discussion of what he calls "intellectual" and "emotional" symbols, "intellectual," or what we would probably call,
"traditional" symbols, Yeats believes, evoke ideas alone, or ideas
mixed with emotions. But "emotional" symbols are distinguished
by their ability to evoke a more indeterminate yet nonetheless
definite quality: "If I say 'white' or 'purple' in an ordinary line of
poetry, they evoke emotions so exclusively that I cannot say why
they move me; but if I bring them into the same sentence with
such obvious intellectual symbols as a cross or a crown of thorns, I
think of purity or sovereignty." [44]

Ignoring for the moment whether it is possible for any word
used with a conscious awareness of its symbolic possibilities to
evoke a purely intellectual idea, Yeats's discussion of symbolism is
acceptable only up to a point. He assumes that certain words used
in certain contexts will evoke a stock response, but he ignores the
fact that each person will bring to a symbol preconceptions based
on his previous experience. The reaction, therefore, of a botanist
to the word "daffodil" will, no doubt, be somewhat different from
that of a Wordsworth; and, even if we assume a more or less
homogeneous poetry-reading public, the reaction of a person who
has just finished reading Wordsworth's "Daffodils," is likely to be
different from that of a person more familiar with Herrick's poem
on the same subject; for Wordsworth's daffodils suggest perma-
nence; Herrick's, mutability.

Unlike Yeats, Symons was acutely aware of this problem, as
is apparent from his discussion of Mallarmé. In the essay on Mallarmé in *The Symbolist Movement in Literature,* he suggests that
this poet's obscurity is largely due to an obsessive search for words
which evoke an emotional impression without expressing an idea:

Words, he has realised, are of value only as a notation of the free breath of the spirit; words, therefore, must be employed with an extreme care, in their choice and adjustment, in setting them to reflect and chime upon one another; yet least of all things for their own sake, for what they can never, except by suggestion, express. . . . Thus an artificiality, even, in the use of words, that seeming artificiality which comes from using words as if they had never been used before, that chimerical search after the virginity of language, is but the paradoxical outward sign of an extreme discontent with even the best of their service. Writers who use words fluently, seeming to disregard their importance, do so from an unconscious confidence in their expressiveness, which the scrupulous thinker, the precise dreamer, can never place in the most carefully chosen among them. To evoke, by some elaborate, instantaneous magic of language, without the formality of an after all impossible description; to be, rather than to express: that is what Mallarmé has consistently, and from the first, sought in verse and prose.[45]

Later in the essay, Symons gives some indication of the difficulties into which this search had led the poet. He distinguishes the three periods in Mallarmé's poetical development: first, when he wrote such beautiful and clear poems as "Sigh"; the middle period, which Symons considers Mallarmé's finest, where "every word is a jewel . . . every image is a symbol, and the whole poem is visible music," the time of the "Hérodiade" and "L'après-midi d'un faune"; and finally, the last period of darkness and obscurity.[46] Symons' discussion of this last period is interesting, for he recognizes that there is a point where additional refinement would lead only to confusion and not to a state where the symbol stands out, naked and clear, pure evocation. Symons recognizes, therefore, that words cannot be dissociated from one another and that, no matter how hard one may try, it is impossible to use words for their emotional suggestiveness alone. Mallarmé aspired to do so, but he forgot—as did Yeats—that words or phrases which evoked certain feelings or moods in him, might not have the same effect on others; consequently, his "pure poetry" is really nothing more than a personal expression of his psychological processes.

To make the point clearer, Symons puts forward what he thinks was Mallarmé's method of composition—a supposition which, as a matter of fact, has recently been substantiated.[47] Symons assumes that the poet starts with a mental sensation and then allows his imagination to play with the idea until certain definite rhythms begin to materialize in his mind, which bring with them words or phrases in which these rhythms can be heard. However, these expressions will, no doubt, recall in perhaps too vivid detail the physical particularities of the scene, so the poet works over his poem, changing words for color or music until he feels that he has a "flawless unity," a poem which will express the sensation without exploring its physical context. But, by this time, of course, "the steps of the progress have been only too effectually effaced"; and, although the poet can trace the steps back to the original sensation, the reader, coming upon the poem for the first time, finds this impossible. Because different people react differently to psychological stimuli, in this case words, the poem is likely to be meaningless.

As Symons says, you "start with an enigma, and then withdraw the key to the enigma; and you arrive, easily, at . . . frozen impenetrability." [48] In short, though Yeats grandly announced what he felt the poetry of the future ought to be—"a poetry of essences, separated one from another in little and intense poems," the result of "an ever more arduous search for an almost disembodied ecstacy"—it was Symons who seems to have had a greater awareness, at this time at least, of the complexities involved. He realized, as Yeats evidently did not, that a search for "essences" frequently ended in obscurity.

Fortunately, Yeats was a better poet than esthetician; and in his poetry of the time, notably in *The Wind Among the Reeds*, he manages to avoid the dangers implicit in the Mallarméan esthetic. Symons admired the poems in this volume, as he made clear in a particularly flattering review, maintaining that in this book Yeats had become "completely master of himself and of his own resources." [49] Symons also demonstrated his approval of Yeats's poetic achievement by adopting his manifesto of the poetry of the future and by endeavoring to write short imaginative pieces in "wavering, meditative, organic rhythms." He also adopted some of the more obvious mannerisms of Yeats's poetic style. In Symons' *Images of Good and Evil*, for example, a collection of poems published in 1899 and evidently intended as a sort of companion piece to Yeats's collection of essays, *Ideas of Good and Evil*, which included both "The Autumn of the Body" and "Symboism in Poetry," Yeats's influence is unmistakable. In Symons' "The Dance of the Daughters of Herodias," for instance, the dance is used with a consciousness of its symbolic possibilities, and in the same poem the dancer Salome is compared to a tree, a comparison favored by Yeats; [50] in "Stella Maligna," "Rosa Flammea," and "Parsifal," the roses which bloom seem to have been plucked from the Cabbalistic tree rather than picked up from where Dowson had flung them; [51] and in such a poem as "The Last Memory" Yeatsian echoes are particularly noticeable:

> When I am old, and think of the old days,
> And warm my hands before a little blaze,
> Having forgotten love, hope, fear, desire,
> I shall see, smiling out of the pale fire,
> One face, mysterious and exquisite;
> And I shall gaze, and ponder over it,
> Wondering was it Leonardo wrought
> That stealthy ardency, where passionate thought
> Burns inward, a revealing flame, and glows
> To the last ecstasy, which is repose?
> Was it Brozino, those Borghese eyes?
> And, musing thus among my memories,
> O unforgotten! You will come to seem,
> As pictures do, remembered, some old dream.
> And I shall think of you as something strange,
> And beautiful and full of helpless change
> Which I beheld and carried in my heart;
> But you, I loved, will have become a part
> Of the eternal mystery, and love
> Like a dim pain; and I shall bend above
> My little fire, and shiver, being cold,
> When you are no more young, and I am old.[52]

In his next volume of poems, however, though entitled *The Loom of Dreams*, suggesting that Symons may have taken his cue from Yeats and resolved to weave his own "cloths of heaven," the influence of the Irish poet gives way to that of John Donne, whom, as we shall see, Symons also regarded as a typical Symbolist poet.[53]

When Symons turned his attention to writers other than those he had discussed in *The Symbolist Movement*, he examines them in the light of his new esthetic philosophy. Just as he had previously come to recognize other elements in some contemporary

French writers which he felt were ultimately more significant than their Decadence, so now he turns his attention to others in the hope of finding a mystical awareness similar to that which he had discovered in the French Symbolists. For example, in an essay on the Italian writer Gabriele d'Annunzio, Symons diverts attention from the more perverse side of his genius to more enduring qualities. He admits that d'Annunzio reminds us "of the reality and the beauty of sensation, of the primary sensations; the sensations of pain and pleasure as these come to us from our actual physical conditions," but he is essentially "the idealist of material things, while seeming to materialize spiritual things," for "he accepts . . . the whole physical basis of life, the spirit which can only be known through the body, the body which is but clay in the shaping or destroying hands of the spirit." [54] Thus, d'Annunzio, for Mario Praz the Decadent prototype, a man who writhed most exquisitely in the delicious pains of the romantic agony, is for Symons above all mystical.

In an article on Oscar Wilde, written at approximately the same time, Symons, who expresses perhaps even more emphatically his indifference to Decadence for its own sake, criticizes Wilde primarily for his lack of sincerity, or what Yeats would have called his lack of "intensity." The title of the essay itself is significant— "An Artist in Attitudes: Oscar Wilde"; and, as one might guess, Symons suggests that Wilde lacked mystical awareness. "His mind was eminently reasonable," he writes, "but of the purely poetical quality he had almost nothing"; therefore, "his style, even in prose, becomes insincere, a bewildering echo of Pater or some French writer, whenever he tries to write beautifully. Such imagination as he had was like the flickering of light along an electric wire, struck by friction out of something direct and hard, and, after all, only on the surface." Wilde, in short, had no desire to penetrate to a higher intensity; instead, he "made for himself many souls, souls of intricate pattern and elaborate colour, webbed into infinite tiny cells, and the home of a strange perfume, perhaps a poison," and then played with them like a juggler. As a result, says Symons, Wilde will not be remembered as a great English writer but simply as "the supreme artist in intellectual attitudes." [55]

Symons also finds Dowson inadequate, and although willing to recognize his "exquisite sensibility," criticize him for his lack of "outlook," his inability to "triumph over the flesh." He "flung roses, roses, riotously with the throng; . . . but it was as one who flings roses in a dream, as he passes through an unsubstantial throng," and so the "depths into which he plunged were always the waters of oblivion, and he returned forgetting them." [56]

Symons did not, however, confine himself solely to his contemporaries, as a cursory glance through *Figures of Several Centuries* testifies. He also considered, among others, such writers as St. Augustine and John Donne, both whom he regards as essentially Symbolist. In writing of St. Augustine, Symons tells us that he felt "intimately the beauty of all things human," and he desired to "pass through these to that passionate contemplation which is the desire of all seekers after the absolute, and which, for him, was God." Thus, when Symons passes final judgment on *The Confessions*, although he admits that St. Augustine speaks only of those things which he thinks God will be interested in and leaves unsaid those things which might have interested men more, the saint does remember nevertheless "everything which the recording angel, who is the soul's finer criticism of itself, has already inscribed in the book of the last judgement." [57]

Symons, who also has high praise for John Donne, finds in him qualities similar to those of St. Augustine. Donne too "winnows all this earthly passsion to a fine fruitful dust to make bread for angels"; he too approaches God through an earnest and passionate contemplation of natural phenomena. However, unlike the saint, the poet appears to Symons as a man of restless, unsatisfied curiosity who constantly speculated upon the facts of existence and was never quite at peace with himself until he came at last to accept the tenets of the Christian religion. Evidently Symons conceived Donne to be similar to himself, and he might almost have used the following passage to describe his own temperament as well as Donne's: "He searches, nothing satisfies him, tries everything in vain; finding satisfaction in the Church, as a haven of rest. Always it is the curious, insatiable brain searching. And he is always wretchedly aware that he 'can do nothing constantly.'"

On the other hand, Donne seems to share with Symons' idol, Verlaine, a capacity for "passion," a view of the world characterized by its brutal intensity; and, no doubt, had Symons been writing about Donne a few years earlier, he would have called him a "Decadent." [58] Now, of course, he is a Symbolist because this restless, intense search through the world of physical appearances had led him to an apprehension of the unknown; he was, in short, in Yeats's words, "an individual of great emotional intensity" who had managed "to follow the pilgrims as it were to some unknown shrine." [59]

III *Critic of the Dance*

Yeats's words aptly describe Symons himself, and it is possible to trace the progress of his spiritual enlightenment through his criticism of the dance. From the time he came up to London from the West Country, Symons had been a devotee of the music-halls; and they soon became such a passion for him that Yeats could refer to him in 1892 as a "scholar in music-halls as another man might be a Greek scholar or an authority on the age of Chaucer." [60] Sir William Rothenstein also recalls, less kindly but just as significantly, that Symons would hold forth at the Crown about his latest acquaintance in the Corps de Ballet: "As people are sometimes vain about their smart friends and their intimacy with the great, so Arthur Symons was elated at knowing, however distantly, any of the dancers at The Empire or The Alhambra." [61]

But Symons' passion for the ballet was really more sincere than Rothenstein's remarks suggest. He found in this art form perpetual delight and constant nourishment for his esthetic sense, as is clear from an essay he contributed to *The Savoy,* in which he commented upon the Degas-like qualities of the Alhambra ballet when viewed from the wings of the theater.[62] Nevertheless, it is equally clear that Symons found the ballet erotically stimulating, for his description of a visit he paid to Nini-Patte-en-l'Aire's "école du chahût" in 1892 focuses on the "depraved virginity" of La Mélinite, the seeming ingenuousness of La Goulue, and the detached, ironic Nini herself, whom he describes as the "Maenad of the Decadence." [63]

Something of Symons' weakness for the perverse fascination which dancers held for him also comes through in his most successful poem, "Javenese Dancers," which must have been inspired by his first visit to Paris during the International Exposition in 1889, where the Oriental troupe was the rage of the season:

> Twitched strings, the clang of metal, beaten drums,
> Dull, shrill, continuous, disquieting;

> And now the stealthy dancer comes
> Undulantly with cat-like steps that cling;
>
> Smiling between her painted lids a smile,
> Motionless, unintelligible, she twines
> Her fingers into mazy lines,
> The scarves across her fingers twine the while.
>
> One, two, three, four glide forth, and, to and fro,
> Delicately and imperceptibly,
> Now swaying gently in a row,
> Now interthreading slow and rhythmically,
>
> Still, with fixed eyes, monotonously still,
> Mysteriously, with smiles inanimate,
> With lingering feet that undulate,
> With sinuous fingers, spectral hands that thrill
>
> In measure while the gnats of music whirr,
> The little amber-coloured dancers move,
> Like painted idols seen to stir
> By the idolators in a magic grove.[64]

The undulating, seductive movements of the dancers constitute the primary fascination, yet it is interesting to note that even here, where Symons responds sensually to the picture he describes, he is also aware that the dancers suggest something other than the erotically stimulating. At the beginning of the poem, the dancer is "catlike" but recognizably human. She smiles "between her painted lids," and then the other dancers glide forth, moving together like inanimate beings, their lack of relationship with the human world emphasized by the suppression of the personal pronoun in stanzas 3 and 4. In the last four lines of the poem the transformation is complete, and the dancers are "painted idols" in a "magic grove," watched by their "idolators." They have transcended human existence and created a mysterious world of their own. Thus, in this poem, although Symons himself was perhaps not even aware of it, the dancers take on a symbolic as well as a sensual significance.

There is another instance of Symons' ambivalent attitude to the erotically stimulating in an unpublished notebook entitled "The Symphony of Snakes" (in the Symons Collection at Princeton) in which he attempts (with only partial success) to impose a symphonic structure on his impressions of the reptiles in the Jardin des Plantes.[65] In both these instances, it would seem that, although Symons was, as he was so fond of saying, "a man for whom the visible world exists," he nonetheless had a latent desire to transcend the actual; and, even during his Decadent phase, he was by no means simply a sensualist.

Only later, however, does Symons seem to have consciously striven to move beyond the external circumstance of the ballet, as for example, in his poem "The Dance," which appeared in *Amoris Victima*, and which was written when Yeats and Symons were living together in Fountain Court:

> For the immortal moment of a passionate dance,
> Surely our two souls rushed together and were one,
> Once, in the beat of our winged feet in unison,
> When, in the brief and flaming ardour of your glance,
> The world withered away, vanishing into smoke;
> The world narrowed about us, and we heard the beat
> As of the rushing winds encompassing our feet;
> In the blind heart of the winds, eternal silence woke,
> And, cast adrift in our unchainable ecstasy,
> Once, and once only, heart to heart, and soul to soul,
> For an immortal moment we endured the whole
> Rapture of intolerable immortality.[66]

Perhaps the most striking feature of this poem is the way it draws upon ideas and images more commonly associated with Yeats. The image of the two dancers whirling together until they become one is evidently a variation of Yeats's gyres; there are appropriately rushing winds, which herald apocalypse here as well as in Yeats; and their destiny, "the blind heart of the winds," is analogous to Yeats's vortex. Indeed, what Symons seems to be describing is the equilibrium of the Thirteenth Cycle, particularly as Yeats describes it in his notes for the first version of the *Vision:* "All whirling [is] at an end, and unity of being perfectly attained. There are all happiness, all beauty, all thought, their images come to view taking fullness, to such a multiplicity of form that they are to our eyes without form. They do what they please, all [struggle] at an end, daimons and men reconciled, no more figures opposing one another in a demoniac dance, and it is these who create genius in its most radical form and who change the direction of history." [67]

In "The Dance," Symons has come to view the dance as essentially symbolic, but he was to give perhaps most explicit expression of the transcendental possibilities of the image in an essay called "The World as Ballet," first published in *The Dome* in 1898, but later included as the epilogue to *Studies in Seven Arts*, his volume of essays. In this short prose piece Symons first speculates upon the origins of the dance, recalls how "from the first it mimed the instincts," and then asks us to consider ballet in the theater, where the dancers "under the changing lights, so human, so remote, so desirable, so evasive, coming and going to the sound of a thin, heady music which masks the rhythm of their movements like a kind of clinging drapery, they seem to sum up in themselves the appeal of everything in the world that is passing, and coloured, and to be enjoyed; everything that bids us take no thought for the morrow, and dissolve the will into slumber, and give way luxuriously to the present."

This definition, of course, is a more precise one of the attitude Symons had previously held; but, in considering the dance not simply as a microcosm of life but as an evocation of another, more ambiguous state, he puts forward a theory very similar to that on which he had based his discussion in *The Symbolist Movement*. Because this world is little more than an illusion, "we are consumed with this hunger to create, to make something for ourselves, of at least the same shadowy reality as that about us." And as there is "something in the particular elegance of the dance, the scenery; the avoidance of emphasis, the evasive, winding turn of things; and above all, the intellectual as well as sensuous appeal of a living symbol, which can but reach the brain through the eyes, in the visual, concrete, imaginative way," the ballet comes close to "the modern ideal in matters of artistic expression." In the dance, writes Symons, echoing Yeats's poetic manifesto in "Symbolism in Poetry," there is nothing "stated, there is no intrusion of words used for the irrelevant purpose of describing; a world rises before one, the picture lasts only long enough to have been there: and the dancer, with her gesture, all pure symbol, evokes, from her mere beautiful motion, idea, sensation, all that one need ever know of event. There, before you, she exists, in harmonious life; and her rhythm reveals to you the soul of her imagined being." [68]

IV *"The Dance of the Seven Sins"*

In Symons' writing of these years, we constantly catch ideas and echoes of Yeats; although one can never be sure who is influencing whom, Yeats was probably the dominant figure in the relationship. Nevertheless, one should not be too hasty in assuming that Yeats was master and Symons merely the eager and intelligent pupil. After all, Yeats did admit in his *Autobiography,* that he owed a lot to Symons.[69] Specifically, in relation to the dance, Frank Kermode has shown that the symbolic use of the dance was part of a common Romantic tradition, going back through Huysmans and Wilde at least as far as Gustave Flaubert and Gustave Moreau; and both Symons and Yeats had used it in their poetry before 1893, when, one may assume, the two men became more closely acquainted.[70] It seems most likely that Symons and Yeats realized simultaneously that the dance image could be invested with greater significance than either had previously been aware of. Certainly, it was only after Fountain Court that both poets made serious attempts to exploit the dance's symbolic possibilities. It was only in "Rosa Alchemica," which initially appeared in Symons' own *Savoy,* that Yeats first attempted to ritualize the dance; and it became after that an increasingly important symbol in his system.[71] Similarly, as has been shown, it was only after Symons had met Yeats that he too began to see in the dance something other than a vaguely erotic suggestiveness.[72] Nevertheless, as Richard Ellmann has maintained, it seems most likely that Symons learned more from Yeats than Yeats learned from his friend.[73]

Even so, both men certainly gained much from the relationship, and it was fortunate that their close association came when it did. During the early years of the 1890's Yeats was constantly seeking a more effective way to express his vision; and Symons, as has been noted, appeared to have reached a point where development along Decadent lines was virtually impossible. It is curious, too, that it was 1895, which Max Beerbohm chose to mark the end of the Beardsley period;[74] and it was, of course, the year of Oscar Wilde's trial and subsequent downfall. Decadence had had its day; the hard gem-like flame had consumed the butterflies that had brushed too close; and, although Symons (as Paul Elmer More has intimated) seemed on the verge of becoming a victim himself, his friendship with Yeats gave him a new stimulus, a new line of development.

However, for Symons the change was not easy. He was, as he put it in the preface to *The Symbolist Movement*, "so meshed about with the variable world and the too clinging appearance of things, so weak before the delightfulness of earthly circumstance";[75] and, as is usual with such people, death was an ever-present physical reality. Thus, although much of his writing at this time seems to minimize the importance of the real world, we feel constantly that this is wishful thinking rather than an expression of an actual state of mind. The conclusion to *The Symbolist Movement*, which makes the final assertion that Symbolist literature reconciles man more readily with death, an idea which Richard Elmann finds so curious,[76] is surely a brave attempt to suggest a resolution to a very real personal fear.

Turning to "The Dance of the Seven Sins," a poem included in *Images of Good and Evil*,[77] we again feel Symons' inability to reconcile his mystical longings with his obstinately earth-bound flesh. Although a rather dreary dialogue between the Soul and the Body, "The Dance of the Seven Sins" is interesting insofar as it shows Symons' almost desperate attempt to affirm the insignificance of this world in favor of the next. The first speaker of this interlude is the Body, who calls for dancers, but is reminded by the Soul that

> All is vain.
> We live, and living is the pain
> We die of while we live. The earth
> Was made in some celestial mirth,
> Not for our pleasure. I, who seem
> To have some memory of a dream,
> I know not when, I know not where,
> Dream not, remember, and despair.

However, the Body is not impressed; it repeats, somewhat peremptorily, its request for the dancers. When they appear, they are the seven deadly sins, who exercise their respective charms and almost succeed in seducing the Body. At the crucial moment, however, the Soul appears to rebuke the dancers, and then asks when the dance "will all be danced through? When will the dawn come?" This questioning prompts a reply from the Stage Man-

ager, who steps forward to announce that it is already dawn. To
which the Soul replies:

> It is. Each morning that decays
> To midnight ends the world as well,
> For the world's day, as that farewell
> When, at the ultimate judgement-stroke,
> Heaven too shall vanish in pale smoke.

Artistically this poem is not very good. The seven dancers receive
too much prominence as they recite their conventional attractions,
and the conclusion, which seems to be making a point, is confused. What Symons appears to be saying, however, is that the
world is only a shadow and ultimately, therefore, is meaningless.
Furthermore, heaven, whose existence can only be apprehended
while we are living in the real world, ceases to be when we die.
Although he had claimed in *The Symbolist Movement* that it was
possible to reconcile oneself with death by recognizing those intimations of another state which are apparent in Symbolist literature, he now seems to regard this idea simply as an illusion, for
with the passing of the body, "Heaven too will vanish in pale
smoke."

This conflict between flesh and spirit became more pronounced
as time passed. Symons wanted to believe in a spirit world, to be
able to affirm with some conviction that the visible world was
indeed but a shadow and that the real intensity would be found in
the next; but the very real circumstances of the all too palpable
world which attracted him so much always made forceful antithetical claims. Perhaps the most interesting feature of "The Dance
of the Seven Sins" is that the rejection of the dancers, which
sounds so theatrical and insincere, is trickled out in Yeatsian finery:

> Now I see
> A wheel turned on an axle-tree,
> A beggar's cloak that the wind shook;
> Your painted faces are a book
> Scrawled by the fingers of a child;
> How is it I was so beguiled,
> What was it that I loved you for,
> O false ones, whom I now abhor
> Even as I did adore you once?

It is almost as if Symons is conscious of not speaking in his own voice and feels obliged to call upon the speech of someone more familiar with fairyland to make his point.

Indeed, most of the poems of this period deal with the desire for transcendence and with the difficulties of achieving this state. For example, in the poem "The Ecstasy," which owes considerably more to Donne than the title, Symons succeeds in lifting "earth into the skies" through the intense emotions aroused by the physical contact of a woman. He acknowledges that his emotion has, in fact, given him a vision of the "glimmer of the gates"; but afterwards there has been a falling away from paradise.[78] Sex may afford release from the world, but the rapture is only momentary:

> When your lips leave my lips, again
> I feel the old doubt and the old pain
> Tighten about me like a chain.
>
> After the pain, after the doubt,
> A lonely darkness winds about
> My soul like death, and shuts you out.[79]

Transcendence, Symons found, was not easily gained. Caught in a conflict between his spiritual aspirations and his resolutely earthbound flesh, he suffered agonies of frustration. Eventually, when escape did become possible, it was only at the expense of sanity.

CHAPTER 4

Arthur Symons: Symbolist: 2

F ROM the date of *The Symbolist Movement in Literature* to the time of his mental breakdown in 1908, Symons produced his finest critical work. His newly found mystical approach to literature provided him with an effective means of discussing all the arts, and from around 1900 he began to investigate the Symbolist possibilities of music, painting, sculpture, architecture, handicraft, dancing, and what he called "the various arts of the stage": acting, production, and stage design. Furthermore, "as life too, is a form of art, and the visible world the chief storehouse of beauty," he undertook to examine places and people from the Symbolist's standpoint as well.

I Critic of all the Arts

In the preface to *Plays, Acting and Music* he outlined these intentions, and also indicated his critical methodology. He insisted that in all his writings about the arts he wished to be "as little abstract as possible" and "to study first principles, not so much as they exist in the brain of the theorist, but as they may be discovered, alive and in effective action, in every achieved form of art." He claimed not to understand "the limitations by which so many writers on aesthetics choose to confine themselves to the study of artistic principles as they are seen in this or that separate form of art," for "each art has its own laws, its own capacities, its own limits," and it "is the business of the critic to distinguish" them. However, "in the study of art as art, it should be [the critic's] endeavour to master the universal science of beauty." [1]

In this new spirit he re-read Pater, and found that he was something more than a perceptive, delicate recorder of exquisite sensations; he had an ethical system of some practical value which he had quietly propounded for the benefit of those who cared to listen. Pater, says Symons,

finds life just worth living, a thing satisfying in itself, if you are careful to extract its essence, moment by moment, not in any calculated 'hedonism', even of the mind, but in a quiet, discriminating acceptance of whatever is beautiful, active, or illuminating in every moment. As he grew older he added something like a Stoic sense of 'duty' to the old, properly and severely Epicurean doctrine of 'pleasure'. Pleasure was never, for Pater, less than the essence of all knowledge, all experience, and not merely all that is rarest in sensation; it was religious from the first, and had always to be served with a strict ritual.[2]

In speaking of Pater's prose style, Symons also shows a greater awareness of its real virtues. No longer does he lavish praise on its langorous delicacy; instead, he points out its effectiveness in reflecting a variety of moods and subjects. Furthermore, says Symons, "what is most wonderful in the style is precisely its adaptability to every shade of meaning or intention, its extraordinary closeness in following the turns of thought, the waves of sensation, in the man himself." [3]

It was, however, in an essay on Richard Strauss that Symons examined in some detail what is probably Pater's most significant contribution to esthetics, one particularly relevant to Symons' own criticism of this time: the theory of the autonomous image. The greater part of the Symons' essay is, of course, concerned with the composer; but, in an interesting preamble, Symons draws attention to that place in "The School of Giorgione" where Pater "comes perhaps nearer to a complete disentangling of the meaning and functions of the arts than any writer on esthetics has yet done," the passage which asserts that "all art constantly aspires towards the condition of music." [4] Symons then states that the music of Strauss attempts to "go backwards from this point towards which all other arts had aspired in vain, and to take up again that old bondage from which music only had completely freed itself."

This approach, says Symons, is surely wrong, because "with the entrance of the 'programme' into music, with the attempt to express pure idea, with the appeal to the understanding to make distinctions, music has at once forfeited all the more important of

its advantages over the other arts, condescending to an equality
which it can never ever maintain; putting itself, in fact, at a wilful
disadvantage." [5] What makes music so perfect an art, he continues, is its direct appeal "to the roots of emotion and sensation";
and, although it is unable to express an idea apart from emotion
and sensation, this limitation is not necessarily a disadvantage,
because in "its infinite reach it speaks the language of a world
which has not yet subdivided itself into finite ideas." As Pater said,
and Symons quotes him, "Art . . . is thus always striving to be
independent of the mere intelligence, to become a matter of pure
perception, to get rid of its responsibilities to its subject or material," and so penetrate to that finer intensity which exists beyond
the senses.[6]

Mallarmé, as Symons had recognized in *The Symbolist Movement in Literature,* had aimed at something similar. He, like
Pater, sought to "evoke, by some elaborate instantaneous magic
. . . without the formality of an after all impossible description;
to be, rather than to express." [7] Yeats too evidently had the same
thing in mind, in suggesting that, "when sound, and colour, and
form are in a musical relation, a beautiful relation to one another,
they become, as it were, one sound, one colour, one form, and
evoke emotion that is made out of their distinct evocations and
yet is one emotion." [8] And Symons also, as is clear from "The
World as Ballet," now conceived the perfect work of art to be a
harmony of forces which defies cerebral analysis yet induces an
emotion analogous to spiritual ecstasy.[9]

This conception of art lies behind all of Symons' mature critical
writing; and, when he suggests in "An Apology for Puppets"—the
introductory essay to *Plays, Acting, and Music*—that real actors in
a play are only a hindrance to communication, he is simply observing to the letter his esthetic creed. He finds human beings
distracting in a play simply because the spectator cannot avoid
responding to them intellectually. As he watches a stage play and
notes the movements and expressions of the actors, he may specu-
late on their private lives, consider their personal appearance, or
in other ways view them apart from the drama they are presenting. The moment he does this, says Symons, the illusion is broken;
and no matter how effective the play may be as a play, it will not
be a beautiful whole.

Consequently, Symons would substitute marionettes for actors in an attempt to avoid distraction from the essential beauty of the presentation because with marionettes one has "personified gesture, and the gesture, like all other forms of emotion, generalised." Thus, the appeal is "to a finer, because to a more intimately poetic sense of things than the merely rationalistic appeal of very modern plays." [10] So it was that Maeterlinck wrote on the title page of his plays, "drames pour marionettes," evidently in an attempt "to intimate his sense of the symbolic value, in the interpretation of a profound inner meaning of that external nullity which the marionette by its very nature emphasizes." So, says Symons, "I find my puppets where the extremes meet, ready to interpret not only the *Agamemnon,* but *La Mort de Tintagiles;* for the soul, which is to make, we may suppose, the drama of the future, is content with as simple a mouthpiece as Fate and the great passions which were classic drama." [11]

Hence, for Symons, the greatest actors are not those who "act," nor yet those who imitate real people in real situations, but those who, as it were, continually reflect the essential mood or spirit of the drama. In an essay on Henry Irving, Symons draws a comparison between him and Eleanora Duse to the latter's advantage, and indicates that they typify the old and the new schools of acting:

To Duse, acting is a thing almost wholly apart from action; she thinks on the stage, scarcely moves there; when she feels emotion, it is her chief care not to express it with emphasis, but to press it down into her soul, until only the pained reflection of it glimmers out of her eyes and trembles in her cheeks. To Irving, on the contrary, acting is all that the word literally means; it is an art of sharp, detached, yet always delicate movement; he crosses the stage with intention, as he intentionally adopts a fine, crabbed, personal, highly conventional elocution of his own; he is an actor, and he acts, keeping nature, or the too close resemblance of nature, carefully out of his composition.[12]

However, Irving does satisfy Symons in his performance of *Coriolanus;* for he is unusually "restrained" and "faithfully interpretative," perhaps a little lacking in energy, which is a fault, but he does avoid "emphasis," which is a positive virtue.[13] Rather similar to Irving is Sarah Bernhardt, who, great though she may be, and invariably is when playing Racine where "everything is subordinate to beauty," nevertheless sometimes fails and then shows her-

self as no more than the "incomparable craftswoman openly la-
bouring at her work." [14]

On the other hand, Réjane is perhaps the actress among all
Symons' contemporaries who comes closest to nature. Unlike
Duse, "who chooses just those ways in which she shall be nature,"
Réjane accepts "things as they are." Thus, though Réjane is unsur-
passed in suggesting the external behavior of the real person in a
real situation, she rarely suggests what Symons would call "the
suffering of a soul." [15] Duse, of course, does, and she is the great
actress whose performance transcends the mere communication of
emotion and becomes instead the expression of a soul. So, in her
performance of *The Second Mrs. Tanqueray*, that "able" but superficial play, she brings to her part "profound tragedy, the tragedy of a soul which has sinned and suffered and tries vainly to
free itself from the consequences of its deeds"; and her masterful
performance only serves to emphasize the deficiencies of the
drama itself.[16] In other words, what distinguishes the really great
actor, as Symons conceives him, is not a meticulous delineation of
the behavior of real persons caught in a particular situation or set
of circumstances, which Réjane manages to perfection, but rather
his ability to suggest a deeper, subconscious interplay of forces.

It is hardly surprising that Symons favors a style of setting and
stage direction which encourages the audience to contemplate the
scene as it would a religious ceremony, rather than to catch at it
hurriedly, forever being forced to readjust its perspective on account of the violent movement of the actors or perhaps the elaborate ingenuity of the scenery itself. In an amusing essay, "On
Crossing Stage Right," Symons comments on the compulsive way
both actors and stage managers in the English theater insist on
movement, apparently feeling that interest will flag unless at least
one person is *doing* something or *going* somewhere.[17]

A similar obtrusiveness is typical of so much contemporary
stage design, whose "real aim is not at the creation of beautiful
pictures, in subordination to the words and actions of the play,
but at supplementing words and actions by the exact imitation of
real surroundings." Far more effective, however, is the art of Edward Gordon Craig, who provides "a symbol instead of an imitation." [18] Symons became a great admirer of Craig, and in an essay
in *Studies in Seven Arts* drew attention to his staging of *The*

Masque of Love, Acis and Galatea, Electra, Venice Preserved, Hamlet, The Masque of London; and speculated upon Craig's probable success if he were to stage Wagner's operas or Ibsen's *Ghosts*.[19] He also considered Craig's theories of stage design as expressed in his *The Art of the Theatre,* noting that Craig shares with Charles Lamb the idea that there are certain plays of Shakespeare which should be read rather than acted, so that the imagination can provide its own illusion, free from the distractions of physical circumstance.

But, says Symons, "an illusion is one thing, a compromise is another, and every art is made up in part of more and more ingenious compromises." What is more, technique, that is to say the means by which a drama is presented, "can be used by the dramatist to his own incalculable advantage," in directing us to the essential meaning of the play.[20] In other words, whereas an ingeniously realistic setting distracts the audience from the dramatist's intention, no scenery at all, except that in the mind of the reader, can, simply on account of its lack of physical limitation, suggest things which the writer never intended. One must seek a compromise, such as Craig's own settings, where the imagination is directed but not controlled.

The function of the actor, the director, and the stage designer is to mediate between the dramatist's vision and his audience. Their responsibility is to present the play as the writer conceived it, but in terms which the audience can understand. Similarly, the dramatist himself, in Symons' theory at least, acts as a medium between the spirit world, whence he derived his vision, and the real world. His function is to translate his vision into language and gesture so that it can be appreciated by his audience. For Symons, there is no essential difference between the actor, the dancer, the musician, or indeed any other kind of artist whose work perishes the moment it is created, and those artists whose work is permanent, inasmuch as it is written down, painted on canvas, hewn from marble or in any other way preserved. Indeed, he suggests that those who perform rather than create are perhaps even greater artists; for there is perhaps something "selfish" in a desire "to perpetuate oneself or the work of one's hands," just as "the more austere saints have found selfishness at the root of the soul's too conscious, or too exclusive longing after eternal life":

To have created beauty for an instant is to have achieved an equal
result in art with one who has created beauty which will last many
thousands of years. Art is concerned only with accomplishment, not
with duration. The rest is a question partly of vanity, partly of business.
. . . Art has to do only with the creation of beauty, whether it be in
words, or sounds, or colour, or outline, or rhythmical movement; and
the man who writes music is no more truly an artist than the man who
plays that music, the poet who composes rhythms in words no more
truly an artist than the dancer who composes rhythms with the body,
and the one is no more to be preferred to the other, than the painter
is to be preferred to the sculptor, or the musician to the poet, in those
forms of art which we have agreed to recognise as of equal value.[21]

This preference Symons expresses for the fleeting impression is,
of course, quite understandable. The products of art which perish
the moment they are created cannot be other than evocative; for,
unlike a poem, painting or piece of sculpture, we cannot re-
examine them at our leisure in order to determine the artist's intentions. Therefore, in order for such ephemeral achievements to
be truly effective, they must make their point simply and clearly;
they must be free from irrelevancy; and their essential quality
must be vividly apparent. Hence, Symons' preference for the
somewhat austere but eloquently simple stage performances of
Eleanora Duse. Similarly, he finds Vladimir de Pachmann preferable to Paderewski: the former "causes wonder," and the latter
"delight." Paderewski is "passionate and human," while Pachmann
is "unhuman and abstract." [22] Finally, Symons even goes so far as
to prefer the more primitive purity of the harpsichord to the
piano.[23]

This is not to say that Symons has come to value classical purity
and restraint for their own sake, although this may seem to be the
case, particularly in his violent denunciation of the tawdry extravagance of the work of contemporary British craftsmen as revealed
in their annual exhibition in London. Symons has no objection to
richness and profusion when they appear to unite in a grand,
symphonic effect. Therefore, although he recoils with horror from
the "blaze of colour, the writhing dragons of form" which claw at
him from all sides at the crafts exhibition,[24] this reaction is not
necessarily inconsistent with his appreciation of Rodin, in whose
sculptures

'Femmes damnées' lean upward and downward out of hollow caves and mountainous crags, they cling to the edge of the world, off which their feet slip, they embrace blindly over a precipice, they roll together into bottomless pits of descent. Arms wave in appeal, they clasp shuddering bodies in an extremity of despair. And all this sorrowful and tortured flesh is consumed with desire, with the hurrying fever of those who have only a short time in which to enjoy the fruits of desire. Their mouths open towards one another in an endless longing, all their muscles strain violently towards the embrace. They live only with a life of desire, and that obsession has carried them beyond the wholesome bounds of nature, into the violence of a perversity which is at times almost insane.[25]

For Symons, this expression of violent physical energy is not Rodin's ultimate appeal. Rodin is a "thinker as well as a seer," and so the world he creates "becomes a world of problems, of symbols, in which life offers itself to be understood," as for example in his version of the Temptation of St. Anthony, which, Symons states, "is the energy of the artist and the solitude of the thinker and the abounding temperament of the man; and it is the triumph of all this in one supreme incarnation, which seems to give new possibilities to sculpture." [26]

And because of Rodin, something new has come into sculpture: it has "learnt to suggest more than it says, to embody dreams in its flesh, to become at once a living thing and a symbol." [27] Therefore, although it may seem that Rodin is preoccupied with superficial realism and sensuous detail, he communicates something more. He finds everything in the world beautiful, "simply because it lives," and his appreciation of life's dynamic force is what he wishes to convey.[28] With Rodin "it is not merely a question of seeing things as they are," but "the more difficult question of getting nature, seen frankly, into the pattern, instead of coming to nature with one's pattern ready made," as Symons wrote elsewhere in relation to contemporary painting.[29] Rodin, who did not impose his view of life on his sculpture, perceived that in nature there was a dynamic force, "the force of the earth, then the two conflicting forces, man and woman; with always, behind and beyond, the secret, unseizable, inexplicable force of that mystery which surrounds the vital energy of the earth itself, as it surrounds us in our existence on the earth." [30] Therefore, like Pachmann,

Rodin is "humbly attentive," endeavoring only to interpret for us the "pattern" which he has perceived. Although it may appear that Symons is drawn to Rodin simply because his figures suggest that their desire has carried them "beyond the wholesome bounds of nature, into a perversity which is at times almost insane," his ultimate appreciation of this artist rests on Rodin's genius in suggesting the very soul of the world in which we live.

In his criticism of Whistler, Symons also gives the impression of having succumbed merely to the more obvious, external, sensuous aspects of his art. Like Rodin's sculptures, Whistler's paintings have an almost Decadent appeal—a foggy wistfulness and a preference for subjects ugly or sordid in themselves—but underlying this is a "pattern," different from Rodin's it is true, but a unifying principle which harmonizes the elements of color and form. Rodin's sculptures reflect the dynamism he perceived in the universe; Whistler saw there no organizing principle at all, so he felt obliged to create one of his own. Yet, in contrast to Watts and Ruskin, great painter and critic though each, respectively, is, both of whom attach "moral values to lines and colours," Whistler was not imposing an external "pattern" on his paintings. What he did was to draw from the materials he was working with and from within himself the controlling harmony which nature herself had failed to supply. Thus, Whistler, in speaking of one of his harmonies in grey and gold, says that he has placed a black spot in front of the tavern of his pictures because black was needed there, and for no other reason.[31] He did not care to reproduce nature on his canvasses, he sought to remedy her deficiencies by arranging her components to conform to a "pattern" he had instinctively apprehended.

The aim of Whistler, writes Symons, is also "to be taken at a hint, divined at a gesture, or by telepathy," which, of course, was also the aim of both Verlaine and Mallarmé. Like their art, Whistler's too is suggestive, and defies rational analysis. Furthermore, each of his creations is an autonomous whole: he "gives you the picture . . . frankly as a picture." [32] In this respect Whistler's art has close affinities with music, a relationship which he explicitly drew attention to in the titles he gave to his pictures—"Symphony in White," "Harmony in Gray and Green," "Arrangement in Black and Brown," "Caprice in Purple and Gold." In addition, says Symons, when speaking of Whistler's art as a whole, "it is musical

terms that come first to one's mind, and every picture has a purity
of tone like that of the finest violin playing. Sometimes a Giorgione, sometimes a Watteau, comes to one as if in exchange for
music; Whistler always." [33]

It is curious that Whistler, the painter of dull fogs and twilights,
should have his pictures likened to "the purity of tone like that of
the finest violin playing," and one might quite justifiably question
the validity of Symons' comparison. Whistler does achieve a harmony in his work, but not by reason of a subtle arrangement of
delicate shades such as one might find in Watteau; instead, he
uses the simpler method of blurring outlines and tones until they
all but melt into an indefinable vapor. There is harmony, no
doubt, but surely not "purity." Furthermore, it is not altogether
true that Whistler presents a picture "frankly as a picture." Swinburne had attacked him for being false to this principle in his
portraits of Carlyle and his mother,[34] and Whistler himself was
liable to undermine his own theories by contradiction. He would
maintain that his paintings were autonomous wholes, existing
simply in their own right; and yet he could also rhapsodize over
twilight on the Thames, which makes it seem that he chose this
subject most frequently because it had a romantic fascination for
him.[35] In his ambition to see all art through Symbolist glasses,
these inconsistencies seem to have escaped Symons, and he singles
out Whistler as the supreme artist, the one who has fused dispa-
rate elements into a beautiful, autonomous unity.

Symons also seems to have felt that Verlaine and Whistler had a
great deal in common. Both aimed at a vague effect, which by its
very vagueness could not fail to be evocative; and both attempted
to produce in their work a condition of music. To Symons, these
artists evidently represented the peak of creative achievement.
But, and this is perhaps significant, the spirit in which he writes of
both Mallarmé and the painter Monticelli seems to indicate that
Symons found in them qualities which almost made them superior.

For example, he had written about Mallarmé at the end of his
essay on that poet in *The Symbolist Movement:*

Symbolism, implicit in all literature from the beginning, as it is implicit in the very words we use, comes to us now, at last quite conscious
of itself, offering us the only escape from our many imprisonments. We

find a new, an older, sense in the so worn out forms of things; the
world, which we can no longer believe in as the satisfying material
object it was to our grandparents, becomes transfigured with a new
light; words, which long usage had darkened almost out of recognition,
take fresh lustre. And it is on the lines of that spiritualising of the word,
that perfecting of form in its capacity for allusion and suggestion, that
confidence in the eternal correspondences between the visible and the
invisible universe, which Mallarmé taught, and too intermittently prac-
tised, and literature must now move, if it is in any sense to move
forward.[36]

Similarly, although Symons speaks highly of Whistler, when in the
same essay he goes on to discuss Monticelli, we wonder whether
he does not in fact prefer Monticelli for seeming to embody
Pater's remark about all art aspiring to the condition of music
even more effectively than his beloved Whistler:

All his painting tends towards the effect of music, with almost the same
endeavour to escape from the bondage of matter; which happens, however, to be the painter's proper material, while it is not the musician's.
Monticelli is scarcely at all dependent on what he sees, or rather he
sees what he likes, and he always likes the same thing. He tries to
purify vision to the point of getting disembodied colour. Other painters
have tried to give us the spiritual aspect of colour. He seems to paint
listening. Confident, doubtless, in the symbolism by which a sound, a
colour, or an emotion may be identical, the expression only being different, not the thing expressed, he hears colour upon a fiery orchestra of
his own. And some of the formlessness of his painting undoubtedly
comes from that singular confidence of his that the emotional expressiveness of music, together with its apparent escape from formal
reality, can be transferred without loss to the art of painting.[37]

What is clear, however, is that there is a strong similarity between Symons' approval of Monticelli and his admiration of Mallarmé: both artists tried to "purify" vision as far as possible. But in
spite of the high praise he accords these artists' intentions, he appears not to have been quite so enthusiastic about their actual
practice. The reason for his disapproval is clear enough: neither
artist took into consideration the limitations of his medium. Mallarmé tried to use words all but devoid of their intellectual mean-
ings, which was foolish, because words just can not be used in this
way; and, as a result, his poetry fails to communicate. Similarly,

Monticelli endeavored "to escape from the bondage of matter; which happens, however, to be the artist's proper material," and he so comes very close to presenting simply color, rather than the color of something, and his paintings, like Mallarmé's poems, are on the point of being incomprehensible. In other words, as Symons recognized in his preface to *Plays, Acting and Music,* "each art has its own laws, its own capacities, its own limits"; and both Mallarmé and Monticelli had gone beyond the resources of their respective arts. Whistler, however, did not; he pushed the potentialities of color and line as far as they would go without lapsing into unintelligibility.

Like Whistler, only on a much grander scale, Wagner succeeded in unifying several different elements and in making from "their distinct evocations" one "emotion." In his essay on the composer, Symons first considers Wagner's theory in some detail, noting that he believed that the greatest art would be a fusion of the genius of Shakespeare and Beethoven; and, in the process of joining these, "all the other arts, those arts not derived directly from man but shaped by man from the stuff of nature, will find their place, as they help towards one result." [38] But this is not to say that opera, as it was known before Wagner's time, is the answer. On the contrary, "unity can be secured only when the expression fully renders the content, and renders it unceasingly; and this can be done only when the poet's aims and the musician's expressions are so blended that neither can be distinguished from the other." So, in the final result, the orchestra will guide "our whole attention away from itself as a means of expression, and direct it to the object expressed." In a sense the music will not "be heard at all, but will become an art that conceals art." [39]

Wagner's theories were embodied in the *Ring der Niebelüngen* and applied practically in the theater at Bayreuth, where he had the orchestra submerged out of sight and a series of proscenium arches constructed, to draw the view of the audience into a vortex—a technique, says Symons, analogous to Whistler's practice of having his "easel pictures thrown back into the depths of the frame." Thus, "in Wagner, the musician, the poet, the playwright, the thinker, the administrator, all worked to a single end"; and in his works one finds the most effective fusion of the arts to make a single, unified and beautiful whole. [40]

Just how effective Wagner's efforts were in practice, Symons

estimates in his "Notes on Wagner at Bayreuth," maintaining that
Parsifal, as performed there, is the "most really satisfying performance" he has ever witnessed in a theater. The great achievement of this opera is that it not only draws upon several arts to
communicate the artist's vision, but actually makes over again another art: " 'Parsifal' presents itself as before all things a picture.
The music soaring up from hidden depths, and seeming to drop
from the heights, and be reflected back from shining distances,
though it is, more than anything I have ever heard, like one of the
great forces of nature, the sea or the wind, itself makes pictures,
abstract pictures; but even the music, as one watches the stage,
seems to subordinate itself to the visible picture there. And, so
perfectly do all the arts flow into one, the picture impresses one
chiefly by its rhythm, the harmonies of its convention." [41]

But the picture is not merely imitative, a representation of the
real world; instead, it is a "symbol of the inner life," an expression
of "the soul of things." And so, "The melody which circumscribes
itself like Giotto's O is almost tangible a thing as a statue; it has
almost contour. But this melody afloat in the air, flying like a bird,
without alighting for more than a moment's swaying poise, as the
notes flit from strings to voice, and from voice to wood and wind,
is more than a mere heightening of speech: it partakes of the nature of thought; it is the whole expression of the subconscious life,
saying more of himself than any person of the drama has ever
found in his own soul." [42]

In summation, Symons—judging by his criticism of Rodin,
Whistler, and Wagner—clearly believes that a great work of art is
a composition of forces shaped by the artist into a "harmony," and
possessed of an "intensity," to quote Yeats, "in which one discovers something supernatural, a stirring as it were at the roots of
the hair." Or to put it another way, great art has a "soul." It reveals a "pattern," which may be intuited but not analyzed and
which expresses what Symons called in his essay on Wagner, "the
subconscious life." The total design will not be an arbitrary arrangement, nor will it be an expression of the personality of the
creator. Even Whistler, who seems to organize the elements in his
paintings to conform to a preordained plan, is really "humbly attentive" to a kind of ideal harmony which he endeavors to communicate through the medium of paint and canvas. Moreover,
great art speaks to the audience in understandable, though inde-

finable terms, evoking in us a definite response; its message may be vague but it will not be unintelligible.

Such a theory, as Graham Hough has pointed out in his essay on Whistler in *The Last Romantics,* is the first step towards a deliberately abstract art, where the artist will arrange his materials to conform to a definite pattern, but will not evoke the forms of nature for justification.[43] If, as Whistler said, he placed a black figure in front of the tavern simply because black was needed there, it follows that it is not really necessary to make the mass of color look like a figure at all—the color itself should be sufficient. Whistler himself did not make this step, neither did Rodin nor did Wagner. In each of these instances the artists maintained fairly close contact with the natural forms of things. Whistler's "Battersea Bridge," for example, is still recognizably a bridge; Rodin's figures are clearly human; and Wagner's librettos make sense when read, while his music is recognizably melodic and his settings not too far removed from the familiar.

Symons was perhaps slightly more adventurous, and could under certain circumstances demand something approaching abstract form, as his criticism of acting, stage design, and handicraft make apparent. But even he was careful not to reject the security of the familiar and the immediately known. "A man for whom the visible world exists," he was never quite at ease when called upon to relinquish his hold on the palpable forms of earthly circumstance: temperamentally, he was quite unsuited for the role of abstract artist.

But there is another reason why Symons failed to accept total abstractionism, a reason implicit in his criticism of both Mallarmé and Monticelli. The moment one moves away from a representation which the normally sensitive spectator cannot equate with natural forms, the chances of his projecting a purely personal vision are increased. In other words, although Mallarmé probably intended to communicate a vision which would evoke a sympathetic response, he—in attempting to refine his language to the point where it would suggest merely the abstraction—fell victim to his private subconscious, assuming that what he found there would be understood by all. Abstraction, Symons appears to have felt, is acceptable in those arts where one can support it by an appeal to external authority—the words an actor speaks, for example, which will make apparent the meaning of his gestures; the stage design of Edward Gordon Craig which becomes meaningful within the context of the play itself; and the work of the craftsman which should conform to its functional pattern.

II *The Limitations of Impressionism*

In a sense the Impressionistic critic, such as Symons, is also a Symbolist artist; for he attempts to suggest the special quality of the work he is considering, just as the artist himself strives to present a "pattern" he has perceived in nature or has drawn from the materials he is using. As such, the Impressionistic critic has a heavy responsibility; and his genius is similar to that of the artist himself. In a short essay on Impressionist writing, Symons defines the qualities of the Impressionist in some detail:

The first thing is to see, and with an eye which sees all, and as if one's only business were to see; and then to write, from a selecting memory, and as if one's only business were to write. It is the interesting heresy of a particular kind of art to seek truth before beauty; but in an impressionistic art concerned, as the art of painting is, with the revelation, the recreation, of a colored and harmonious world, which (they tell us) owes its very existence to the eyes which see it, truth is a quality which can be attained only by him who seeks beauty before truth. The true impressionist may be imagined as saying: Suppose I wish to give you an impression of the Luxembourg Gardens, as I see them when I look out of my window, will it help to call up in your mind the impression of those glimmering alleys and the naked darkness of the trees, if I begin by telling you that I can count seven cabs, half another at one end, and a horse's head at the other, in the space between the corner of the Odéon and the houses on the opposite side of the street; that there are four trees and three lamp-posts on the pavement; and that I can read the words "Chocolat Menier," in white letters, on a blue ground, upon a circular black kiosk by the side of the second lamp post? I see those things, no doubt, unconsciously, before my eye travels as far as the railings of the garden; but are they any essential part of my memory of the scene afterward?

Then he informs us that the danger for the Impressionistic critic is the same as that which confronts all Symbolist artists: in a search for "beauty" before "truth," he may give us something which may be a distortion of it.[44]

Symons' own work is not altogether free from this kind of critical subjectivity, as can be seen in *Cities*. He seems to have been a little defensive about the book from the beginning. In the Introduction, dedicated to Madame la Comtesse de la Tour, Symons reminds us again that he is "one of those for whom the visible world exists, very actively," and so he has felt the impact of certain cities perhaps more strongly than the average traveler, and has even grown "to hate some of them intensely." [45] It seems, then, in the light of this statement, that the following pages are to be little more than "a kind of subjective diary"—the reflection of Symons' own sensations while staying in the places he described. But, he says, such is not the case. Even though "it is so much easier to put oneself into things than to persuade things to give up their own secrets," he would rather "aim at this difficult kind of truth." [46]

Just how successful Symons was in this last attempt is not altogether clear. The fact that he wrote the Preface at all, perhaps indicates that he was a little uncertain of his success; and we know that Yeats disapproved of the book as a whole, maintaining that "a writer might be excused for seeking a soul in Venice, Seville or Rome," but not, in Symons' case at least, in Moscow.[47] It is also worth remarking that four years later Symons selected those essays he had written about Italian cities, added several more, and published a new volume called *Cities in Italy;* and he resolved at the same time not to reissue *Cities* in its original form,[48] which is probably additional evidence of his dissatisfaction with his failure to live up to the intention expressed in his earlier dedication.

Clearly, some of the essays in *Cities* reflect Symons' rather special temperament as much as the city he is writing about. Such is the essay on Moscow, which Symons visited during the summer of 1897 with Havelock Ellis—the hottest summer for thirty-seven years, apparently, which caused Symons so much physical discomfort that it influenced his attitude to the city. Thus Symons recalls only one positive impression of his stay, the cool, quiet seclusion of the Strasnoi Convent, where Moscow and "its noise and heat, seemed shut off by a veil of quiet." [49] Naples, too, traditionally associated with peasant gaiety, sunshine, and raw animality, filled Symons with terror, especially its "long streets of tall mean houses" and its "gross, contentedly animal life huddled away in its midst, like some shameful secret." [50] Life in the raw always repelled Symons; it had to come to him suitably veiled in mystery before he could really appreciate it. Neither Moscow nor Naples did that, and apparently Symons' feelings got the better of him.

It is not often, however, that Symons allows his private sensibilities to interfere with the essential truth of his theme, in spite of the fact that such adulteration is almost inevitable in Impressionistic criticism. In the criticism of his later years Symons' personality does intrude, but certainly at this time it is surprising how faithfully Symons is able to reproduce the nuance and flavor, "the subconscious life" of the subject he describes. T. S. Eliot attacked Symons for failing to keep his personality out of his criticism of Baudelaire, but the fault, he finds, is not so much Symons' as that of Impressionistic criticism itself. Eliot admits that Symons, "if anyone, would be said to expose a sensitive and cultivated mind—cultivated, that is, by the accumulation of a considerable variety of impressions from all the arts and several languages—before an 'object'." Eliot adds that in Symons' criticism one would expect to find exhibited to us, "like the plate, a faithful record of the impressions, more numerous or more refined than our own, upon a mind more sensitive than our own." But, taking as his test case Symons' essay on *Antony and Cleopatra,* "the question is not whether Mr. Symons' impressions are 'true' or 'false'. So far as you can isolate the 'impression', the pure feeling, it is, of course, neither true nor false. The point is that you can never rest at the pure feeling. . . . The moment you try to put the impressions into words, you either begin to analyse and construct, to *ériger en lois,* or you begin to create something else." [51]

Eliot is surely right; and it is curious that, although Symons had been so perceptive in finding that it was just this which made Mallarmé's last poetry so unsatisfactory, he failed to see its possible implications in Impressionistic criticism. Certainly he was alive to the dangers of substituting personal likes and dislikes for an objective view; and he asked only that the critic should "find out for us more than we can find ourselves," [52] but he seems to have been completely unaware of the basic incongruity of the Impressionistic critic's position. For the most part Symons avoided this dilemma by writing about only those artists and places whose character seemed most closely akin to his own—Verlaine, Huysmans, Whistler, Pater, Florence, Seville—or with whose esthetic philosophy he could sympathize. Thus Symons was able to write a

particularly good book on William Blake, which perhaps did more
to clear away the prejudice and confusion surrounding this writer
than any other work on Blake before this time.

III *Symons and Blake*

Blake had not been treated very kindly by his contemporaries.
Robert Hunt, one of the few people who had even noticed him,
considered his paintings a "farrago of nonsense, unintelligibleness
and egregious vanity, the vivid effusions of a distempered
brain";[53] but, as the years passed, Blake found more sympathetic
critics. G. F. Tatham was kind, if unperceptive;[54] and Alexander
Gilchrist's biography, which appeared a few years later, supplied
some much needed information about the poet's life, although it
did little to clarify the obscurity of his work.[55] To all these writers
Blake was primarily a painter and an engraver, and it was not
until Swinburne's long essay on him that there was any real attempt to grapple with the poetry, particularly with the prophe-
cies.[56] In 1874, William Rossetti published a volume of Blake's
poems, together with an appreciative memoir, which adds little to
our understanding of the poet;[57] and it was not until the famous
three-volume Yeats-Ellis edition of the complete poems that there
was a systematic attempt to unravel some of the complexities that
had baffled previous critics.[58]

Without doubt the Yeats-Ellis edition is a major landmark in
Blake criticism, for the editors realized that there was, after all,
some coherence to the Blake myth and that it was "no mere freak
of an eccentric mind, but an eddy of that flood-tide of symbolism
which attained its tide-mark in the magic of the Middle Ages." [59]
However, in spite of Virginia Moore's enthusiastic praise for
Yeats's and Ellis' investigations, whose "detailed commentary,"
she claims, "has never been refuted, though it has often been ignored," [60] the real significance of the work must rest on its approach rather than on its conclusions.

Far more successful than the textual apparatus of the Yeats-
Ellis edition are two essays on Blake which appeared in Yeats's
Ideas of Good and Evil, both of which stress Blake's importance
in relation to art and literature rather than to "magic." In one of
them, "William Blake and the Imagination," Yeats refers to Blake
as a "Symbolist who had to invent his symbols": a man "crying out
for a mythology, and trying to make one because he could not find

one to his hand." Thus, Blake's obscurity is a result of his arbitrary choice of symbols, and Yeats suggests that Blake might have fared better had he been able to draw upon a familiar symbology such as the Catholic religion, Old Norse mythology, or the traditional lore of Ireland.[61] Nevertheless, as Yeats points out in "William Blake and His Illustrations to the *Divine Comedy*," Blake was a great artist, the first of modern times "to preach the indissoluble marriage of all great art with symbol," a man who realized that the only way one could express "some invisible essence" was through the medium of Symbolism.[62]

Symons, of course, had pointed to the importance of the French Symbolists, justifying his high opinion of them in similar terms. Thus Yeats's more recent estimate of Blake, based less on his role as a messenger from the occult world than his importance as a representative of true poetry, seems to have been the product of his association with Symons. However, if Symons was responsible for bringing home to Yeats the significance of Blake in relation to French Symbolism, Yeats in his turn almost certainly stimulated Symons' interest in Blake—but Yeats was not solely responsible for Symons' interest in the visionary poet. Symons, from his earliest years an ardent admirer of Blake, had composed in 1884 some well-meaning though rather callow verses to him, later included in an essay called "Notes on Romani Rai." Artistically, Symons' poetic eulogy is only this side of execrable, but it shows his youthful enthusiasm for the poet, and, particularly, his desire to transcend the forms of external circumstances, which was evidently rooted in him at an early age.[63] In the same essay Symons refers specifically to John Sampson who, like Symons, was himself deeply interested in gypsy lore and whose edition of Blake's poems in 1906 seems to have provided the incentive for Symons' own study of the poet.

Even so, Yeats's enthusiasm for Blake must have been an important factor in reawakening Symons' interest in him during the latter part of the 1890's, for in numbers three, four, five, and six of *The Savoy* there are reproductions of some of Blake's designs, and in three, four, and five Yeats had written articles on his art.[64] Furthermore, in 1896, when Symons and Yeats were together in Ireland and when Symons was writing a reply to his detractors in the Preface to the second edition of *London Nights*, a passing reference to Blake comes easily to him.[65] However, it was not

until after 1900 that Symons' poetry began to show obvious signs
of Blake's influence, and it was not until 1907 that his influence
became dominant, as evidenced by the poems bearing that date in
Knave of Hearts (1913).

The most Blakean of all Symons' poems in this collection are
undoubtedly those grouped under the title, "The Brother of a
Weed." [66] The fourth in the series demonstrates Symons' dependence most noticeably:

> Why is not sorrow kinder to all these
> That have short lives and yet so little ease?
> Life is but anxious fear to lambs and hens,
> And even birds are enemies of men's
> Because they rob a cherry-tree; the mole
> Cannot be kept in quiet in his hole
> Though he is softer than a velvet gown;
> The caterpillar is soon trodden down
> Under a boot's ignorant heel, though he
> Is woven finer than old tapestry.
> The worm is close and busy and discreet,
> The foe of no man living: no man's feet
> Spare him, if he but crawl into the sun.
> Who can be happy, while these things be done?

It is not simply that this poem recalls *The Songs of Innocence
and Experience* in its concern for such lowly creatures as lambs,
worms, caterpillars, and so on; the series as a whole is based on
Blake's assumption, expressed in "The Marriage of Heaven and
Hell," that "everything that lives is holy." [67] Furthermore, the
idea running through these poems recalls the underlying theme of
Songs of Innocence and Experience: the fall from an unthinking
innocence to recognition of the suffering creatures in the world of
experience. In the first poem of the group, Symons declares that
he has shut up his soul against the world:

> And I have never wondered that my sight
> Should serve me for my pleasure, or that aught
> Beyond the lonely mirror of my thought
> Lived, and desired me. I have walked as one
> Who dreams himself the master of the sun,
> And that the seasons are as seraphim
> And in [*sic*] the months and stars bow down to him.

But later he says:

> I will get down from my sick throne where I
> Dreamed that the seasons of the earth and sky,
> The leash of the months and stars were mine to lead,
> And pray to be a brother of the weed.

And, finally, with renunciation comes pity for the suffering creatures around him, which leads him to question why it is "that the joy of living gives/Forgetfulness to everything that lives?"

It is clear that Blake was frequently in Symons' mind around the turn of the century, so it is not surprising that in 1907 he should have written a full length study of the poet, especially as Yeats's essays had emphasized Blake's affinities with a literary movement about which Symons knew a great deal. However, unlike his other literary criticism of this time, which is simply Impressionistic criticism, although in the best sense of that term, his essay on Blake makes some claim to be considered also as genuine literary scholarship. Symons was evidently familiar with previous Blake criticism, such as the works mentioned earlier, and also with more recent studies as Edwin Ellis' *The Real Blake,* and, of course Sampson's edition of Blake's poetry, whose text he quite rightly prefers to that of the Yeats-Ellis edition.[68] Although Yeats no doubt stimulated Symons' interest in Blake, and probably helped him to a greater understanding of the poet, Symons had also done some research on him himself.

Thus, although we may reasonably assume that Symons was deeply indebted to Yeats for his understanding of Blake, he does not lean on him for support; instead, he seems particularly aware of his friend's lapses, as in his treatment of Yeats's rather curious theory that Blake was of Irish descent. Yeats believed that true poetry of the kind he had described in "Symbolism of Poetry" had survived in Ireland; and, if Blake could also be made to seem Irish, Yeats himself would be regarded as the proper heir to the true poetic tradition. Yeats's attempt to turn Blake into a Celt was supported by evidence tenuous in the extreme; and, although it was left to a later scholar to explode completely the myth of Blake's Irish ancestry,[69] Symons does a fairly successful demolition job himself.

He presents the two theories of Blake's lineage—one by Alfred S. Story, who maintained that Blake was connected with a Wiltshire family of that name, and the other, Yeats's own, which suggested that Blake's father was Irish, originally called O'Neil. Yeats believed him to have changed his name from O'Neil to Blake after he married Eileen Blake; and at the same time, O'Neil's son by a previous marriage also changed his name and settled in London, while a son of the more recent union went off to live in Malaga.[70] Symons, who goes to some trouble to establish documentary evidence for both these theories, is forced to conclude that both are founded on hearsay. He admits to having corresponded with a Mr. Martin J. Blake, "the compiler of the Blake family records," in an effort to throw some light on the problem, refers to some of Sampson's remarks on the same subject, cites a relevant entry in Crabb Robinson's *Diary*, and notes that he has consulted the parish register—all with a view to settling the question, concluding that the theory of Blake's Irish ancestry is extremely unlikely to say the least.[71]

As for the book as a whole, there is a fairly well integrated account of Blake's life with his work. Symons does not make the mistake, which most of his predecessors had, of separating the significance of the poetry from that of the painting; moreover, Blake does gain in intelligibility by being placed in the tradition of the French Symbolists. Like the French Symbolists, Blake refused to accept the strictures of conventional morality, and Symons finds no "moral tendency" in his poetry, for the only sin that Blake recognized was the sin of negation.[72] Blake comes even closer to the Symbolists in his belief in the mystical transcendence of the arts: in his view that art ought not be representational, for observation is one of the daughters of Memory, and Blake had no use for Memory—only Imagination.[73] Finally, in noting that Blake in his illustrations used color not to suggest a factual representation but rather for its symbolic significance, Symons suggests that Blake painted as an Impressionist would, using color "with a definitely musical sense of its harmonies." [74]

Symons also quotes four lines which for him succinctly express Blake's vision:

> For double the vision my eyes do see
> And a double vision is always with me.
> With my inward eyes, 'tis an old man grey,
> With my outward, a thistle across the way.

But, in suggesting that Blake recognized only the symbol and refused to admit the reality, Symons seems to feel that Blake failed
to achieve the double view to which he aspired.[75] It is interesting
to note, too, that, however much Symons may have applauded
Blake's esthetic intentions, Symons himself also found it difficult
to view external phenomena with his "inward" and "outward"
eyes simultaneously; but, where Blake's "outward" eye sometimes
failed him, Symons' "inward" eye most frequently lapsed. He
wanted desperately to enjoy both a spiritual and an earthly paradise; but, try as he might, he could rarely transcend the latter.

Symons stated his dilemma most forcefully in a poem called
"Felpham" dated 1903:

> Here Blake saw the seventy-seven
> Stairs, and golden gates of heaven;
> He said, 'Come, for heaven is there';
> He saw heaven where I see air,
> He saw angels where I see
> Only divine earth and sea.
> 'Bread of thought and wine of delight,'
> Fed his spirit day and night,
> But what heavenly bread or wine
> Shall in these late days feed mine?
> What strong lust of mortal eyes
> Shuts me out of Paradise?

But, says Symons, "I can see, and 'tis enough/For my appetite of
love"; and he describes the beauty of the scene before him, dwelling on the rich coloring of the "green grass/Brighter than clear
crysopras," and the "tufted tamarisk that is/Ruddier than burnt
topazes." [76] Thus, Symons suggests that his single vision is perhaps preferable to Blake's, whose "meaning is no longer in the
ordinary meaning of the words he uses." To understand Blake we
must read him "with a key, and the key is not always in our hands;
he forgets that he is talking to men on the earth in some language
he has learnt in heavenly places. He sees symbol within symbol,
and as he tries to make one clear to us, he does but translate it into
another, perhaps no easier, or more confusing." [77] In short, like
Mallarmé's, Blake's imagination "is in rebellion, not only against
the limits of reality, but against the only means by which he can
make vision visible to others." [78]

IV   Spiritual Adventures

The difficulties of the artist's position, his special vision, and his problem of communicating at all adequately what he sees interested Symons immensely; and his volume of short stories, *Spiritual Adventures,* is, for the most part, concerned with just that. In a sense, the contents of this volume are not stories at all but "imaginary portraits," as Symons himself called them.[79] They are psychological enquiries into the "souls" of certain persons of sensitivity and refinement, all of whom are, in one form or another, extensions of Symons' own personality.

The first story, "A Prelude to Life," is evidently a factual account of Symons' early years, suggested perhaps by Pater's "The Child in the House." The narrator speaks of his solitary upbringing in Cornwall; the absence of sympathy between him and his father, and his inability to understand fully his frail, submissive mother; his love of literature; his determination to make a career in letters, and his coming to London to make good that resolve; and, finally, his passion for the music-halls—all of which quite accurately describes Symons' own childhood and adolescence.

Another tale, "The Autumn City," which has for its main character Daniel Roserra, an exquisite connoisseur, "who tended his soul as one might tend some rare plant," [80] and who made the mistake of introducing the woman he loves to his favorite city, is probably Symons himself, perhaps recounting a real experience, while the city itself, Arles, is certainly one of Symons' favorites. In another tale, Henry Luxulyan falls in love with the disfigured Baroness Eckenstein; he is not drawn to her by a grand passion but by an intellectual fascination of the kind Yeats criticized Symons for in his chapter on the "Lost Generation" in his *Autobiography.*[81] In "Esther Kahn," the heroine's calculated acceptance of a liaison with Philip Haygarth in the hope that the experience will perfect her performance as an actress is also typical of Symons, who took great care to acquire a wide range of experience, believing that only in this way could the artist achieve the fullness of vision necessary to his vocation.

However, the two most significant tales—at least in terms of Symons' own esthetic position—are "The Death of Peter Waydelin" and "Christian Trevalga." Both stories have much of Symons in them; both express an artistic doctrine with which

Symons would sympathize; and both emphasize the penalties the sincere artist must pay for a glimpse of the intensity it is his business to communicate.

Peter Waydelin's theory of art is typical of the Symbolist artist as Symons conceives of him, but more specifically he seems to have had in mind Toulouse Lautrec, Beardsley, Whistler, and Degas, whose personalities or esthetic doctrine find expression in the story.[82] Waydelin is mainly concerned with the sordid, but he distills from it a vision which is nonetheless beautiful. In a series of conversations with the narrator, Waydelin puts forward his philosophy of art: once, when they are lying on the beach somewhere between Bognor and Felpham; and, later, in the sordid surroundings of Waydelin's home in Islington. He says first:

All art, of course . . . is a way of seeing, and I have my way. I did not get to it at once. Like everybody else, I began by seeing too much. Gradually I gave up seeing things in shades, in sub-divisions; I saw them in masses, each single. It takes more choice than you think, and more technical skill, to set one plain colour against another, unshaded, like a great, raw morsel, or a solid lump of the earth. The art of the painter, you observe, consists in seeing in a new summarising way, getting rid of everything but the essentials; in seeing my patterns. You know how a child sees a house? Well, that is how the average man thinks he sees it, even at a distance. You have to train your eye not to see. Whistler sees nothing but the fine shades, which unite into a picture in an almost bodiless way, as Verlaine writes songs almost literally 'without words.' You can see, if you like, in just the opposite way: leaving in only the hard outlines, leaving out everything that lies between. To me that is the best way of summarising, the most abbreviated way. You can get rid of all that molle, sticky way of work which squashes pictures into cakes and puddings, and of that stringy way of work which draws them out into tapes and ribbons. It is a way of seeing square, and painting like hits from the shoulder.[83]

He points out that he has never done anything which is not beautiful because he has never done anything which is lacking in life, "and life is the source and sap of beauty." So, even his paintings of vulgar women behind the footlights of a second-rate music hall, which appear perhaps to be ugly, really are not. Unfortunately, the average person must know, first of all, whether such and such a thing is supposed to be beautiful before he will either praise or condemn it. He will find beauty in a flower but not in a weed, and for that reason, says Waydelin, "I hate nature, because fools prostrate themselves before sunsets; as if there is not much better drawing in that leaf than in all the Turners of the sky." [84]

Later, when the painter is close to death in the miserable place he has chosen for his home, he speaks of the role of the artist in relation to his work; and he asks whether one should be as thorough in one's life as in one's drawing. Certainly, he had been thorough:

I made the music-halls my clubs; I lived in them, for the mere delight of the thing; I liked the glitter, false, barbarous, intoxicating, the violent animality of the whole spectacle, with its imbecile words, faces, gestures, the very heat and odour, like some concentrated odour of the human crowd, the irritant music, the audience! I went there, as I went to public-houses, as I walked about the streets at night, as I kept company with vagabonds, because there was a craving in me that I could not quiet. I fitted in theories with my facts; and that is how I came to paint my pictures.[85]

More specifically, Waydelin later refers to the influence of Japanese painting, because in it there is a "new kind of reality," and he took it as his guide:

I will get at the nature of this artificial thing, at the skin underneath it, and the soul under the skin. Watteau and the Court painters have given us the dainty, exterior charm of the masquerade, woman when she plays at being woman, among 'lyres and flutes.' Degas, of course, has done something of what I want to do, but only a part, and with other elements in his pure design, the drawing of Ingres, setting itself new tasks, exercising its new technique upon shapeless bodies in tubs, and the strained muscles of the dancer's leg as she does 'side-practice.' What I am going to do is to take all the ugliness, gross artifice, crafty mechanism, of sex disguising itself for its own ends: that new nature which vice and custom make out of the honest curves and colours of natural things.[86]

Waydelin, committed to penetrating to the essence of truth, is the ideal Symbolist artist. His esthetic position lies somewhere between Bognor, "where nature deals with its material so much in the manner of art," and Blake's Felpham, where nature is sacrificed in favor of the spirit world it evokes. Like Beardsley and Lautrec, both of whom Symons had in mind when creating Peter

Waydelin, and like Rodin, Wagner, and Verlaine, of whom the same thing might also be said, the artist accepts the materials of this world but is not content merely with expressing the apparent, outward forms of things. Instead, he wishes to arrange the materials in his composition to suggest a basic idea, the "subconscious life" of the world in which we live.

Waydelin, of course, pays the supreme price for his sincerity and for the absoluteness with which he pursues his aims. The life he chooses wears him down until he does; but, even in his last moments, he is conscious of his calling as an artist, asks for his sketch-book, and attempts to capture the spirit of his wife's tear-stained, over-painted face.[87] The point Symons makes is that the price of dedication and sincerity is self-annihilation. The death of Waydelin is not at all an indictment of the way he chose to live, nor even of the way he chose to realize his esthetic aims; it is, quite simply, the inevitable conclusion, the sacrifice the true artist is forced to make in return for his vision.

If "The Death of Peter Waydelin" emphasizes the tragedy of the artist who feels confident in being able to project his vision, "Christian Trevalga" is concerned with the predicament of the artist who, like Blake, Mallarmé, and Monticelli, rebelled against "the limits of reality." Again there is much of Symons in the portrait, although he has noted that Vladimir de Pachmann was his main inspiration.[88] Like the author, Trevalga had an unhappy, solitary childhood; knowing little affection from his parents, he is unable to give any; a sensitive child, he escapes from the restrictive demands of social intercourse into a room at the top of the house where he can play his piano undisturbed, in much the same way that Symons sought refuge among the books of his "study."[89] Like Symons too, Trevalga comes to think more of his art than of people: "The emotion of the music, the idea, the feeling there, that was what moved him; and his own personal feelings, apart from some form of music which might translate them into a region where he could recognise them with interest, came to mean less and less to him, until he seemed hardly to have any personal feelings at all."[90]

Soon the external world in which Trevalga moves begins to have less and less significance for him. The only woman who could arouse an even faintly human response leaves him, tired from trying to break through to his heart. Alone, he concentrates more and more on his art; and at last he begins to hear music all around him, wherever he goes, "ravishing sounds in the air, a music which was like what Chopin might have written in Paradise," far sweeter music than he could ever coax out of the keyboard. But it was the end: "he awoke enough to realise that they thought him mad; and it was with a very lucid fear that he waited now for the doctor who was to decide finally whether he might still keep his place in the world." [91] Finally, he is committed to an asylum where he dies five years later.

The fate of Christian Trevalga foreshadowed Symons' own with tragic accuracy; for, while vacationing in Italy in 1908, he too went insane and was obliged to enter an asylum. The nature of Trevalga's madness was also remarkably similar to Symons'. After pursuing his musical studies with a neurotic intensity, Trevalga heard beautiful music everywhere; Symons, after an unfortunate love affair with Lydia and a period of intense literary activity, undertaken, in part, to satisfy the extravagant demands of a wife he had married in 1901,[92] also had hallucinations, experiencing strange and sometimes melancholy visions of surpassing beauty. In a poem written in October, 1907, and dedicated to Vladimir de Pachmann, Symons describes the sensations stimulated by the music of Chopin:

> The sounds torture me: I see them in my brain;
> They spin a flickering web of living threads,
> Like butterflies web of living threads,
> Nets of bright sound. I follow them, in vain.
> I must not brush the least dust from their wings:
> They die of a touch; but I must capture them,
> Or they will turn to a caressing flame,
> And lick my soul up with their flutterings.
>
> The sounds torture me: I count them with my eyes,
> I feel them like a thirst between my lips;
> Is it my body or my soul that cries
> With little coloured mouths of sound, and drips
> In these bright drops that turn to butterflies
> Dying delicately at my finger-tips? [93]

And later, only a few days before he went insane, he visited a concert in Venice, describing its effect on him for the readers of

his music column in the *Saturday Review,* and conjuring up morbid and enigmatic visions of the soul of that city:

. . . what strange and obscure secrets you conceal! Crimes and car-
nality of the Doges, the horrible Council of Ten, the dungeons under
the 'Bridge of Sighs,' a water prison, where men languished without
hope, heard the tides, loud and menacing voices going on eternally
with a monotonous plash on the marble walls of the dungeon. They
are dark cells, a torture-room, rusty chains and bolts and bars, chains
just long enough to enclose an ankle or two wrists, chains long enough
to enclose the body in a permanent inaction against the wall. There is
an odious beauty in these relics of time when cruelty was a virtue and
Casanova was a spy. Inexplicable soul of Venice, Satan threw dice with
God and won half the game. Inexplicable soul of beauty, heroic soul,
ignorant, empty, indifferent, enigmatical soul. . . .[94]

In his autobiographical account of his madness, *Confessions: A
Study in Pathology,* Symons describes other bizarre visions of this
time, but, he asks, was this really madness? Might not his so-
called hallucinations be really a keener, more perceptive view of
reality similar to that of Gérard de Nerval's?

[His] genius, to which madness had come as the liberating spirit,
disengaging its finer essence, consisted in a power of materialising
vision, and without losing the sense of mystery, or that quality which
gives its charm to the intangible. Madness in him had hit, as if by
lightning, the hidden links of distant and diverging things, in somewhat
the same fashion as that in which a similarly startling sight of things is
gained by the stimulus of haschisch, by which vision is produced, while
the soul, sitting safe within the perilous circle of its own magic, looks
out on the panorama which either rises out of the darkness before it
or drifts from itself into the darkness.[95]

After all, John Clare, another poet whom the world had called
mad, had actually written his best verse when he was insane. His
"lyrical faculty" took flight when his contact with the external
world was at its lowest point. At this time "a new joy [came] into
his verse, as if at last he [was] at rest," and "because his mind
[was] in a kind of oblivion of everything else; madness being, as
it were, his security." [96]

In other words, Symons endeavored to look upon his madness
as vision, as an experience which enabled him to penetrate to that
intensity which had for so long lain just beyond his grasp. How-

ever, as Blake and Mallarmé, and perhaps Monticelli too, had discovered before him, as Christian Trevalga had found out, Symons too was to learn that communication of such vision was virtually impossible. Nerval succeeded, it is true; and, according to Symons, Coleridge too almost managed it, at least in "Kubla Khan," where he came nearer to the "absolute" than "in any other existing poem," to that "ideal of lyric poetry which has only been lately systematized by theorists like Mallarmé." [97] But Symons, although he tried his hand at poetry, painting, and music while he was in the asylum, was never able to express at all satisfactorily the patterns and sensations that teemed in his brain.

Symons had, of course, been aware of the problem of communication in the past, when he had maintained that "all art is a compromise," but now the disparity between his visions and their physical embodiment in those art forms in which he tried to express them, made the problem seem even more acute. It seemed to make the artist an even more isolated figure than he had perhaps been willing to admit. Mallarmé had failed to come to terms with the world, and as a result his work was little known and less understood; Blake was unable to make the necessary compromise between the world of his imagination and the world in which he moved, and was ridiculed; Christian Trevalga too, an isolated figure most of his life, became even more estranged from first his friends and then all normal people as his vision intensified; and now Symons as well was made to feel more vividly than ever before that the artist and society were not simply different from one another but antithetical. As he wrote in *Confessions:*

The artist, it cannot be too clearly understood, has no more part in society than a monk in domestic life; he cannot be judged by its rules, he can neither be praised nor blamed for his acceptance or rejection of its conventions. Social rules are made by normal people for normal people, and the man of genius is fundamentally abnormal. It is the poet against society, society against the poet, a direct antagonism; the shock of which, however, it is so often possible to avoid by a compromise. So much licence is allowed on the one side, so much liberty foregone on the other. The consequences are not always of the best, art being generally the loser.[98]

Symons had learned that he also had to pay the penalty for vision; in his case madness, from which he never fully recovered.

CHAPTER 5

Arthur Symons and the Twentieth Century

AFTER one and a half years Symons had recovered sufficiently from his mental breakdown to take his place once more in the normal world; but, although his doctors pronounced him cured, Symons' hold on reality seems to have been faint. Jessie Conrad, for example, recalls how Symons and her young son John became good friends and how one day, when the poet arrived at their house in one of his more mystical moods, the two walked about the house, eventually coming to a moat full of muddy water, which Symons suggested that they try walking on. Fortunately, young Conrad was of a practical turn of mind and agreed only on condition that Symons tried first.[1]

Indeed, the impression we have of Symons during these years is of a frail, delicate creature, quietly meandering through the world, unmoved and untouched by reality, living with his memories, and either forgotten or ignored by the rising generation of literary men. John Betjeman, for example, who recalls seeing him at the Café Royal, a favorite haunt of his earlier years, was prompted to record the event with a few lines in the Café manager's autograph book:

> I saw him in the Café Royal,
> Very old and very grand.
> Modernistic shone the lamp-light,
> There in London's fairy-land.
> Devill'd chicken, devill'd whitebait,
> Devil if I understand
> Where is Oscar? Where is Bosie?
> Have I seen that man before?
> And the old one in the corner
> Is it really Wratislaw?
> (Scent of tutti-frutti-sen-sen
> And cheroots upon the floor.)

On that day Symons stood at the door of the Brasserie, looking around to see if there was anyone there he knew; but, says, Betjeman, "he knew no one except for whoever it was with him. I don't think anyone spoke to him." [2]

Other glimpses of Symons during these years are provided by Sylvia Beach, who recalls a visit Havelock Ellis and Symons made to Shakespeare and Company during the 1920's;[3] and William Rothenstein, who caught sight of him at a concert by Yvette Guilbert in the 1930's, was surprised to find him still alive, so fragile had his health been for so long.[4]

I   *Dreamer*

However, for all his fragility and apparently frail grasp of reality, Symons' literary output was almost as prolific as it had been previous to his breakdown. Unfortunately, interesting though some of his original writing is, and perceptive as a few—a very few—of his critical observations are, the greater part of his work is feeble, rambling, and undistinguished. Most of it gives the impression of having been written in a dream, a dream world of the past. His criticism is more personal reminiscence than comment, and the comments usually are restatements of what he has said before; his original work is, for the most part, extremely mannered, outmoded, and at times incredibly bad. With only one or two exceptions, Symons' writings after 1908 add nothing favorable to his reputation. If they have any significance at all, it must be for the light they throw on his temperament rather than for their qualities as literature.

When Symons had written *Silhouettes* and *London Nights,* he had chosen subjects and themes which were, to the late nineteenth century at least, rather shocking. The poems in these volumes were redeemed, however, even at their worst, by a certain grace and facility, and always there lay behind his verses a cool, relatively detached persona. In the poetry which Symons wrote after 1908, although they are similarly dedicated to the erotic and the perverse, the tone is considerably more violent, and in many cases the delicate artistry is quite lacking. Such titles as "Jezebel Mort," "The Seeds of Vice," "The Snake Soul," "The Serpent," "At the Morgue," "Nero," "The Adder," "Salome," "Cleopatra," give some indication as to the subjects which attracted Symons during these later years.[5]

In addition there are eight poems loosely grouped under the title "Studies in Strange Sins," another group of seven called "For des Esseintes," a larger collection dedicated "To Lesbia," and several more from Catullus, "chiefly concerning Lesbia." [6] Even poems with innocent sounding titles frequently mask contents of rather startling perversity. This is "Sonnet," for example, from *Lesbia and Other Poems* (1920):

> Why is it that you use your fascination
> Of fatal beauty that has power to ensnare
> Even the serpents in their violation
> Of all that's sane in webs of woven hair,
> And sets them into deeds of vile sedition
> As rebels round a city mutinous
> That fall into the folds of their perdition
> And are for that more subtly poisonous?
> To do all evil and to do no good,
> As a pure virgin in her first confession
> Lets out the secret of her innocent blood
> Nor sees in the hidden monk behind the grate
> A conscience-stricken face consumed with hate.[7]

This is a far remove from the poems of *Silhouettes* and *London Nights*. The dispassionate worldliness of the sophisticated observer gives way to the tortured involvement of the hysterical victim; the conscious, deliberate craft gives way to confused and passionate utterance.

The vicious destructiveness of sensual desire is the theme of another late poem, "The Chimera: Notre Dame":

> The Chimera created by the Eternal Hours,
> Seized by the perverse passion of Rabelais,
> Disguised in Satan of the Eternal Towers
> Of Notre Dame that rule the night and day,
> Himself destructive, his own self devours
> His living flesh, this Bird of Evil Prey,
> Lean as a Lenten Monk, nor rains nor showers
> Ever refresh: his one Desire to slay
> The misbegotten child that the First Sin
> Conceived from the body of primeval Lust;
> Only his eyes, that see but from within,
> Hooded and clawed, his feet grind down the Dust.[8]

In "Song of the Fire," from the same collection, Symons goes further, and seems to have adopted an almost medieval attitude to the flesh, suggesting that an excess of passion leads only to annihilation.[9] He recognizes the force of the temptations to which the flesh is subject, but he also insists that surrender brings with it damnation. This theme is even more obviously stated in Symons' very late poetry, none of which has been published but is preserved in the Symons Collection at Princeton. "Sin" is a fairly typical example:

> What is Primeval in the world is Sin,
> And Sin is as Elemental as Primeval.
> Sin entered the World and with lust did Sin begin
> To sin, and always the Eternal Devil
> Excites and agitates the Flesh; then enters in
> The Serpent's venom. In the Medieval
> Times Sin was rampant and the Monkish skin
> Was stung by sweet poison. Woman incarnate Evil,
> Since Lilith, is the Temptress, and her Mesh
> Can be as slimy as the Serpent's Flesh.
> And without Sin the world would be unexistant.
> That is man's verdict. Adorable and accursed,
> She can satiate and she can extinguish our thirst,
> And accursed, and adorable, She is persistent.[10]

Clearly, these pieces demonstrate that Symon's days as an effective poet are over. Preoccupation with the allurements of the flesh and the sinfulness of sensual desire are now Symons' dominant (one might say, only,) themes. Constantly, he reminds us that the flesh is weak; that the temptations it must bear are strong; and that surrender can only mean damnation. The language, too, of these later poems becomes increasingly biblical; the tone, oratorical; and together with the typographical peculiarity of capitalizing certain key words, everything points to the inescapable conclusion that Symons' early Methodist upbringing has reasserted itself. Arnold B. Sklare has said that Symons' mental collapse was probably a result of his inability to reconcile Epicurus with Wesley; and, however oversimplified such a diagnosis may be, it appears to be essentially true.[11]

This is not to say that Symons enacts the age-old story of the youthful sinner who at last repents and seeks once more the forgiveness and all-embracing love of the church he had previously rejected. Just as there had been something factitious about Symons' earlier flirtation with Decadence, so his reawakened Puritanism appears similarly artificial. In his youth Symons was constantly ridiculed by his contemporaries on account of his shrill pleas on behalf of madder music and stronger wine. Lionel Johnson, for example, in some critical estimates of his fellow Rhymers, recognized Symons' poetic talent but found his subject matter both fatuous and offensive, and not a little insincere:

A singular power of technique, and a certain imaginativeness of conception, mostly wasted upon insincere obscenities. Baudelaire and Verlaine generally ring true, and their horrors and squalors and miseries and atrocities have the value of touching the reader to something of compassion or meditation. Symons no more does that than a tea-pot. 'This girl met me in the Haymarket, with a straw hat and a brown paper parcel, and the rest was a delirious delight: that girl I met outside the music-hall, we had champagne, and the rest was an ecstasy of shame.' That is Symons. And this sort of thing in cadences of remarkable cleverness and delicacy! He can be pleasant and cleanly when he chooses: has written things of power and things of charm. But is a slave to impressionism, whether the impression be precious or no.[12]

William Rothenstein used to say that Symons woke up in the morning with bad intentions and broke them every night;[13] and, when in 1902 Yeats took the young James Joyce and his brother, Stanislaus, to see Symons, after being entertained with stories about Verlaine, Dowson, Lionel Johnson, and Beardsley and an impromptu recital of the Good Friday music from *Parsifal,* Yeats explained to his companions that "Symons had always a longing to commit great sin but [was] never . . . able to get beyond ballet girls." [14] Thus, Symons was far from being the licentious monster he would have liked to have been, and one can understand why Augustus John, with whom Symons became friendly after World War I, was at times irritated by the writer's frequent asseverations concerning the sins of his youth, meeting "with some impatience his high-pitched professions of turpitude." [15]

Inevitably, one feels that Symons would not be gloating over the prospect of damnation if his earlier sins had been as purple as he had painted them. Yet, to dismiss his reawakened sense of guilt as insincere is to do him an injustice. What appears more likely is that Symons' reawakening to the sin-and-punishment syndrome of the Methodist Church is part of his lifelong quest to impose some sort of meaningful structure on his life. Or, to put it another way, Symons seems to have spent his days in a restless quest to establish his identity, to find his "center," and his reversion to Methodism is one of the last stages in that process. He admitted in one of his last books that to him "wandering is the most wonderful thing in the world: the only escape from the crying voices of the nerves, from the body that aches," and is "the only relief for those who have become over-weary of their existence." [16]

Earlier, however, Symons' wanderings seem to have been more purposeful. His restless enthusiasm to know something of all the arts; his study of the literature of several languages; his constant search for new impressions and strange sensations; his anxious pursuit of women of various types and nationalities, all seem to have been part of a quest for personal and spiritual fulfillment. Obscurely aware of the inadequacies and inhibitions of his early religious training, Symons seems to have made an effort to free himself from its restrictive influence and to establish a satisfactory creed to take the place of the old. Decadence turned out not to be the answer, and the mystical way he subsequently chose under the aegis of Yeats led him into a perilous no-man's-land where he suffered the agony of a conflict between his earthbound flesh and his spiritual aspirations. After mysticism, where else could he turn if not to the simplistic faith of his early years? Like Melville's Ahab and Symons' Seaward Lackland of *Spiritual Adventures,* Symons too was a landless being, increasingly tortured by his isolation and self-destructiveness; he searched for peace and was anxious to find something which would at least give him the illusion of fixity in a shifting chaos.

Symons was an alien from the beginning, as a child estranged from his parents, as a young man morbidly aware of his lack of communion with his fellow creatures, and in his last years as an eccentric old man who mystified his Kentish neighbors. He felt his isolation keenly, and from time to time seems to have made rather pathetic attempts to achieve some kind of relationship with things around him and with his wife Rhoda, for example, to whom he wrote a number of revealing letters making clear his desperate need for security and love.[17] In his poem "Amends to Nature," which he dates in his *Collected Works,* "July 24, 1909," but which must have been written earlier, he also gives expression to his feeling of alienation, but maintains that at last he has been able to enter into communion with nature:

> I have loved colours, and not flowers;
> Their motion, not the swallow's wings;
> And wasted more than half my hours
> Without the comradeship of things.
>
> How is it, now, that I can see,
> With love and wonder and delight,
> The children of the hedge and tree,
> The little lords of day and night?
>
> How is it that I can see the roads,
> No longer with usurping eyes,
> A twilight meeting-place for toads,
> A midday mart for butterflies?
>
> I feel, in every midge that hums,
> Life, fugitive and infinite,
> And suddenly the world becomes
> A part of me and I of it.[18]

There is a similar theme in a collection of verses preceded by a long, confessional prose preface in which Symons records his affection for his dog, Api. He describes the animal minutely—its appearance, habits, idiosyncrasies; whom it liked and whom it didn't; and, after its death, the elaborate preparations that were made for its burial. To the insensitive reader, Symons' maudlin account is either distasteful or absurd; but, as he mentions later, Api's death meant more to him than simply the loss of a beloved pet. It was also the destruction of a creature which had succeeded in coming close to his heart, and which had awakened in him a feeling of human sympathy:

For nearly a year I have been normal, human, like other people, no longer isolated from the men and women whom I meet in the street, but with a new feeling of belonging to them by at least one link of friendliness. The link has gone now, and I walk more lonely, in a self-absorption now wholly returned upon itself. Once I had stepped out of myself for my friend's sake; I had gone where he led me, and in loving him I had come to have some little sympathies for other people. Now I put them again out of my heart and out of my mind lest they should bring me memory.[19]

Evidently Api had succeeded where others had failed, drawing Symons out of himself and into communion with others; but, with the death of the dog Symons once more turned inward and sought escape from the intolerable present.

II   *Symons and Baudelaire*

Symons found that his most effective escape was into a world of art. To art he could respond with a sensitivity normally reserved for human beings, without incurring the danger of becoming emotionally involved, thus avoiding an open assault on his deeper feelings. In the past his hyper-sensitivity had led him, more frequently than not, to the essential spirit of the work he was criticizing. After his breakdown, however, Symons seems to have been more interested in seeing through the work to the personality behind it; focussing his attention on those artists with whom he seems to have felt a personal kinship, he impressed his own personality upon them almost as if he felt the need to lose himself in the contemplation of their souls. The result is that such different writers as Baudelaire, Conrad, Rossetti, Swinburne, and Hardy all appear as reflections of himself.

The writer who seems to have impressed Symons most during these years is Baudelaire, a poet no longer regarded simply as the Decadent *par excellence,* but as a serious writer intensely concerned with the nature of man, of sin and suffering, damnation and redemption. As a young man, however, Symons seems to have regarded Baudelaire simply as a poet who dealt in forbidden themes and described them with alluring rhythms and intoxicating turns of phrase. For example, in a poem called "Laus Stellae," published in *Lesbia and Other Poems* (1920), but written in 1889, at a time when he was, on his own admission, under the influence of Baudelaire,[20] there are "tropic flowers of poisonous breath," "spells of Thessalanian sorceresses," "philtres in magic moonlights brewed," and a lady's hair which the poet compares to an

> . . . odorous bower
> Deep-scented as, in seas afar,

The blue and living noontide hour
Washes on the shores of Malabar.[21]

Symons apparently saw in Baudelaire, at this time, little more
than an evocation of the exotic and the perverse, a vision made
doubly attractive by those undulating rhythms and langorous cadences which sound so much more seductive in French than in
English translation.

Three years later, however, Symons was ready to maintain that
Baudelaire was the first "modern" poet, one who was concerned
with sensations and self-analysis, and who pointed the way for
Verlaine.[22] But, in 1899, in *The Symbolist Movement in Literature,* a book which one would expect to deal more fully with the
so-called originator of the modern esthetic, Baudelaire is mentioned only briefly in the introduction, and Symons' remarks there
are not very illuminating. What he seems to be saying is that
Baudelaire is a Naturalist, whose modernity consists only in his
choice of subject matter. Unlike Verlaine and Huysmans, who
also made use of daring themes, Baudelaire makes no attempt to
evoke a transcendental state, and so he necessarily belongs to a
secondary order of writers.[23]

By 1906, however, Symons seems to have revised his estimate of
the poet once more. He draws attention to Baudelaire's discovery
of Poe, Wagner, and Manet; and he suggests that, although Baudelaire is a "romantic," there is something "classic in his modera-
tion." Most interesting of all, Symons calls attention to one aspect
of Baudelaire's genius which had been consistently ignored by his
critics and, hitherto, even by Symons himself: To "cultivate one's
hysteria" so calmly, and to affront the reader (*Hypocrite lecteur,
mon semblable, mon frère*) as a judge rather than as a penitent;
to be a casuist in confession; to be so much a moralist, with so
keen a sense of the ecstasy of evil; that has always bewildered the
world, even in his own country, where the artist is allowed to live
as experimentally as he writes. Baudelaire lived and died solitary,
secret, a confessor of sins who has never told the whole truth, *le
mauvais moine* of his own sonnet, an ascetic of passion, a hermit
of the brothel.[24] This description is certainly accurate enough of
part of Baudelaire's intention; and, although Symons failed to appreciate the poet's tortured cynicism, he does at least recognize

that Baudelaire was considerably more than simply a poet who glorified depravity.

Unfortunately, in Symons' criticism of Baudelaire, written after 1908, whatever understanding he may have had about the poet's cynical self-examination fades before the vision of a poet who surrenders deliciously to the sweets of sin. In both his study of Baudelaire and in the Preface to his collected translations of Baudelaire's prose and poetry, Symons writes of the French poet almost as if he were a typical poet of the decadent 1890's. Gone is the earlier emphasis on Baudelaire's restraint, and instead we have a portrait of a more overtly Satanic Swinburne:

In the poetry of Baudelaire, with which the poetry of Verlaine is so often compared, there is a deliberate science of sensual and sexual perversity which has something curious in its accentuation of vice with horror, in its passionate devotion to passions. Baudelaire brings every complication of taste, the exasperation of perfumes, the irritant of cruelty, the very odours and colours of corruption, to the creation and adornment of a sort of religion, in which an Eternal Mass is served before a veiled altar. There is no confession, no absolution, not a prayer is permitted, which is not set down on the ritual.[25]

In the translations themselves, Symons emphasizes the poet's Decadent qualities, even at the expense of distorting his original. Particularly noticeable is the way Symons invests the most innocent remarks of Baudelaire with a Satanic flavor. In "La Beauté," for example, the lines, "Je trône dans l'azure comme un sphinx incompris," Symons translates, "I throne in the azure with Satan a Sphinx sound sleeping"; "Et jamais je ne pleure et jamais je ne ris," he renders, "Satan has never seen me laughing nor even weeping"; and the line "Mes yeux, mes larges yeux aux clartés éternelles," becomes "Mine eyes, mine eyes immense—Satan's delights." But perhaps the most blatant example of Symons' diabolizing is his rendering of a line from Baudelaire's "Le Tonneau de la Haine," "De ne pouvoir jamais s'endormir sous la table," as "Of never having slept even in Hell." [26]

Apart from this irritating insistence on seeing Baudelaire as a thorough-going Satanist—understandable, certainly, in terms of Symons' later preoccupation with hell and damnation, but hardly justifiable in terms of the material he is translating—the quality of

Symons' translations from Baudelaire is not very high. In rendering Verlaine's poetry into English, he had managed to communicate both the tone and spirit of the French without sacrificing
literal exactness; but in translating Baudelaire, although he keeps
fairly close to the originals, there are frequent lapses into verse of
the most pedestrian kind and sometimes into sheer nonsense. A
fairly typical example is his rendering of "Avec ses vêtements
ondoyants et nacres." Baudelaire had written:

> Avec ses vêtements ondoyants et nacres
> Même quand elle marche on croirait qu'elle danse
> Comme ses longs serpents que les jongleurs sacres
> Au bout de leurs batons agitent en cadence.

> Comme la sable morne et l'azur des déserts
> Insensibles tous deux à l'humaine souffrance,
> Comme les longs réseaux de la boule des mers,
> Elle se développe avec indifference.

> Ses yeux polis sont faits de minéraux charmants,
> Et dans cette nature étrange et symbolique
> Où l'ange inviole se mêle au sphinx antique,

> Où tout n'est qu'or, acier, lumière, et diamants,
> Résplendit à jamais, comme un astre inutile,
> La froide majesté de la femme stérile.[27]

And Symons translates:

> With her vestments irridescent and undulating,
> Even when she walks it seems as if she dances,
> Like those sly snakes the jugglers, strange signs creating,
> Make coil in cadences and then fall in trances.

> Like the dull sand and the deserts and men's fretwork,
> Insensible to suffering and to mere indolence,
> As in the swish and the swell of the waves the network
> Rises, she develops herself with indifference.

> In her eyes one sees the refractions of a jewel,
> And in this symbolical nature mixes and drinks
> The inviolate Angel with the inevitable Sphinx,

> Where all is diamond, light, gold, steel, more cruel
> Than these, the cold majesty of the woman sterile
> Shines everlasting like a star in peril.[28]

Apart from such particular defects as the absurd inclusion of the word "fretwork" (1. 5), simply because it rhymes with the literal translation of "réseau" ("network," 1. 7), the awkwardness of the English "develops herself" (1. 8) for "se développe," the unwarranted insertion of such words as "trances" (1. 4) and "indolence" (1. 6), which suggests a swooning voluptuousness more typical of Swinburne than Baudelaire, Symons manages to blunt the sharpness of Baudelaire's cynicism and to change the whole tone of the poem into something much less disturbing than the original. This is particularly true of the last lines where "la femme stérile," evidently intended by Baudelaire to be symbolic of her environment, is transformed by Symons into a more or less conventional *femme fatale.*

On the whole, the general effect of Symons' translations is to obscure the cosmic implications of Baudelaire's poetry and to intensify the impression that his writing is simply the expression of an abnormal personality who has entered into a pact with the Devil. Instead of Baudelaire's view of man as a forlorn creature tortured by his lust and uncertain of his destiny, Symons makes Baudelaire's poetry seem more the expression of a private sensibility morbidly attracted by sin and corruption.

To say this is to suggest that Symons conceived of Baudelaire's personality as being remarkably similar to his own, and in *Baudelaire: a Study,* for example, the notion that Symons identified himself with Baudelaire is inescapable.[29] Like Baudelaire, Symons too had taken hashish, and he presents his own experiences under the drug as corroboration for the French poet's observations in *Les Paradis Artificiels.* No doubt because Symons, like Baudelaire, had himself experienced the disillusionment of this form of escape, he was moved to make the rather startling judgment that this book "is the most wonderful . . . that Baudelaire ever wrote." [30] Also, Baudelaire was forced to leave Paris to go into exile in Belgium, where he came to appreciate the misery of being alienated from familiar surroundings; Symons, also knew the bitterness of isolation, and whenever Baudelaire writes of his exile, the Englishman nods in understanding agreement.[31]

On a more intimate level, evidently with memories of his own madness in mind, Symons wonders whether Baudelaire had experienced what he himself had felt so acutely only a few years ago. In a letter of February, 1865, Baudelaire had written of his present state of mind which he called "an absolute abdication of the will." "What reason," Symons asks,

was there for him to 'abdicate' the one element in our natures by which we live at our greatest, the very root of our passions (as Balzac said), 'nervous fluids and that unknown substance which, in default of another term, we must call the will?' Man has a given quality of energy; each man a different quality; how will he spend it? That is Balzac's invariable question. All these qualities were always in Baudelaire.

Had he finally, after so many years in which his energy was supreme, lost some of his energy, struggling, as he seems to do, against insuperable difficulties that beset him on either side, like thieves that follow men in the dark with the intention of stabbing you in the back? Does he then try to conjecture what next year might bring him of good or of evil? He has lived his life after his own will: what shall the end be? He dares neither look backward nor forward. It might be that he feels the earth crumbling under his feet; for how many artists have had that fear —the fear that the earth under their feet may no longer be solid? There is another step for him to take, a step that frightens him; might it not be into another more painful kind of oblivion? Has something of the man gone out of him: that is to say, the power to live for himself? [32]

In this passage, probably more clearly than anywhere else, one can recognize what seems to be the greatest attraction of Baudelaire for Symons: their apparent similarity of temperament. It must have seemed to Symons that the unhappy, alienated poet of *Les Fleurs du Mal* embodied so much which he recognized in himself, and, conscious of their supposed affinities, invested his subject with his own innermost fears and aberrations. In Baudelaire Symons found a mirror for his own identity, and the critical judgments he makes concerning the poet reflect his own temperament perhaps even more clearly than his subject's.

Symons also found a kindred spirit in Joseph Conrad, whose work he had begun to admire in 1907, and on whom he had written an article the following year, later rejected by the *Quarterly Review*.[33] What must be the same essay, though perhaps revised, was included in *Dramatis Personae* sixteen years later; and parts of it also found their way into *Notes on Joseph Conrad,* published in 1925. It is an interesting piece of writing, both for the light it sheds on Conrad and also on Symons himself. On the one hand, Symons is inclined to view Conrad as a Symbolist, pointing out that to him reality is non-existent and that he sees "through it into a realm of illusion of the unknown: a world that is comforting and bewildering, filled with ghosts and devils, a world of holy terror." [34] At the same time Symons also writes of Conrad in terms similar to those he uses to describe Baudelaire, comparing him to a "Satanical spider" who discusses human affairs with a "cynical ferocity." [35] In other words, the Conrad essay shows Symons at the half-way stage between *The Symbolist Movement in Literature* and his study of Baudelaire; he is sensitive to Conrad's evocation of the forces which lie behind man's day-to-day existence, but he is more deeply engrossed by the author's supposed cynicism and his Satanical view of humankind.

Briefly, in spite of certain intimations of spirituality, the essay on Conrad gives clear indication of what Augustus John aptly referred to as Symons' "growing prepossession with the lurid and the macabre." [36] Just as in writing of Baudelaire, Symons ignored the more important aspects of his work, so in his evaluation of Conrad he accentuates the novelist's morbid cynicism almost to the exclusion of everything else. If Symons had been able to detect in Browning "a fresh salt wind blowing in from the sea," [37] he should with more literal exactness have found a similar, if fainter, breeze in Conrad. Although Symons was willing to recognize that the novelist shows the heroism in even the worst of men,[38] nevertheless he leaves the reader with the impression that Conrad's spiritual home is not the sea so much as the humid, odiferous jungles of the Malay Archipelago.

What seems to have happened, of course, is that Symons saw his own experience mirrored in the pages of Conrad, just as he seems to have felt its presence in the writings of Baudelaire, leading him to assume that Conrad's personality was akin to his own. Thus, when Symons says later that Conrad "vibrated to every sensation as Verlaine vibrated, as Pachmann vibrates," [39] he could with equal justification have added his own name too. Although Conrad did not altogether appreciate Symons' interpretation of his character as seen through the novels,[40] the two men became close friends, perhaps, as Jessie Conrad suggests, because they were so unlike.[41] On the other hand, they probably had more in common than one would at first imagine. Both shared a sort of brooding intensity; both had made tentative journeys into "the heart of darkness"; both were interested in the nature of the unconscious. They certainly admired each other's work; and, according to Jessie Conrad, Symons' poetry was probably the only verse her husband ever read.[42]

Symons' work on Baudelaire and Conrad is perhaps his most significant of these later years, but he also wrote about many other literary and artistic figures, among them Rossetti, whose paintings revealed his twin obsessions of "beauty" and "women," and whose temperament, as described by Symons, seems closely akin to Symons' own: "The tremulous flame of his soul was disturbed by a mere breath, a sound, a shock on his nerves, and his sensitiveness was so intense that it interpenetrated his work with his life." [43] In Swinburne, Symons found "a certain abnormality, a certain perversity, a certain love of depravity in the highest sense of the word";[44] and he seems to have been disproportionately impressed by Swinburne's novel, *Lesbia Brandon,* presumably because its subject fascinated Symons so much at this time.[45] Finally, in discussing Thomas Hardy, he found congenial that novelist's melancholy view of life and the way he studied "the working of fate or law (ruling through the inexorable moods or humors), in the chief vivifying and disturbing influence in life, women," [46] which, no doubt, called vivid memories of Lydia to Symons' mind.

In Symons' criticism of Baudelaire, Conrad, Rossetti, Swinburne and Hardy, to choose a few of the writers who appear to have impressed him particularly during his later life, his interpretation is not so much erroneous as misleading, and its defects are the result of distortion rather than willful misrepresentation. Although some of Symons' later criticism is interesting because it draws attention to certain aspects of the writer's psychology and temperament, most of it demonstrates all too vividly the disadvantages of the Impressionistic critic's position. There is in this late work, quite simply, too much of Symons' own neurotic sensibility; and, instead of "*la vraie vérité,*" one finds the reflection of the artist's personality. In a sense, this criticism was written more for Symons' benefit than for his readers', for by investigating temperaments similar to his own, he could, as it were, reaffirm his own identity and establish his "center."

This impulse probably accounts for the many digressive anecdotes that find their way into his writing at this time, most of which have more to do with Symons himself than with the writer he is discussing. Typical is an essay entitled "Rimbaud and His Biographer," which begins with a lengthy and irrelevant reminiscence of a visit which Symons paid to Verlaine while the latter was confined to a hospital on the Island of Saint Louis, which in turn prompts other anecdotes of the Parisian 1890's, before Paterne Berrichon, the subject of the essay, is finally introduced.[47]

Admittedly, the tone of all the essays in this collection, *The Café Royale and Other Essays,* is conversational rather than directly informative. Therefore, it is perhaps a little uncharitable to demand from this volume a too high standard of scholarly disinterestedness. Nevertheless, the impression remains that the real subject of the essay is Symons himself and not Paterne Berrichon. Even in other, less esoteric volumes with greater pretensions towards professional standards of criticism, the same element appears. For example, in his study of Baudelaire, Chapter V begins: " 'I am far from sure', said Paul Verlaine to me in Paris, 'that the philosophy of Villiers de l'Isle Adam will not one day become the formula of our century.'" [48] Then Symons goes on for several pages to consider Villiers de l'Isle Adam in some detail, without even mentioning Baudelaire. Again, the apparent reason for the digression is simply that Symons wishes to relive his past and to recall those writers with whom he felt a personal kinship.

Another feature of this later criticism is the inclusion of correspondence from the subjects about whom Symons is writing. The appearance of these letters cannot be accounted for on the grounds that they reflect either the personality of the people who wrote them, or that they make significant comments about their work. They are there simply because they reflect credit on Symons himself and demonstrate his intimacy with the great. Of the letters from Conrad which Symons prints in his short study of the novelist, one praises Symons for his perceptive analysis of the novels, and another praises him for his *"désir de vivre,"* which, says Conrad, is more joyfully alive in him than in most people.[49]

In *Studies in Strange Souls,* the volume devoted to Rossetti and Swinburne, he even prints a letter from Christina Rossetti to Mrs.

William Rossetti, in which she refers to Symons' early poem, "The Revenge." This letter, in fact, tells us nothing about Dante Gabriel, perhaps a little about Christina, but a great deal about Symons himself, who chose for it to appear in print. Christina refers to Symons' poem as "diabolical," and mentions that "its degree of serene skill and finesse intensifies . . . its horror"; and, although she regrets that it was ever written, and hopes that it will never be published, such criticism no doubt pleased Symons, who was always anxious to be thought more wicked than he was.[50] In his book on Eleanora Duse, in a section simply entitled "Duse's Letters," Symons prints correspondence he had received from the actress which tells us little about Duse herself or her art, but they do make clear that some kind of intimacy existed between the actress and the critic, and it is this which Symons is most interested in communicating.[51]

This public demonstration of his friendship with the great is, to repeat, all part of Symons' search for an identity. It was in the company of the leading figures of the 1890's, and those writers who seemed to share their spirit, that Symons felt most at home, so almost all of his major critical writing after 1908 is concerned with calling up their shades in an effort to establish some kind of a link between him and those artists whom he had known so well, or with whom he had something in common. Symons knew that between him and the world in which he lived there existed no great bond of sympathy; his only refuge was, therefore, in a familiar world of the past, or in the company of artists similar to himself.

III   *Symons the Dramatist*

Symons' alienation is dramatized, either consciously or unconsciously, in the plays he wrote during his later years. He had, of course, in his very first volume of poetry revealed an interest in a dramatic form of utterance, for the majority of the poems in *Days and Nights* are dramatic monologues, and George Meredith had predicted that Symons would end by writing verse drama.[52] Many of the poems included in subsequent collections are dramatic studies involving two or more speakers, and in 1892 the Independent Theatre staged a one-act play called *The Minister's Call*, which Symons had adapted from Frank Harris' short story, "A Modern Idyll." [53] However, not until later does he seem to have become really interested in writing plays for the theater; and, although some of his dramas were certainly begun and a few of them completed before 1908, it was only after his breakdown that they were formally prepared for publication.[54]

There is little doubt that Symons' verse dramas are superior to a great deal of his poetry written during the first decade of the twentieth century; and, although most modern critics find little in them to warrant their preservation from oblivion, at least two of Symons' contemporaries believed that they would constitute his major literary achievement. Arthur Waugh maintained that "the spirit of drama is as much alive in them as the spirit of poetry," [55] and T. Earle Welby declared that *The Harvesters* was nothing less than a masterpiece.[56]

A later critic, Priscilla Thouless, writing, incidentally, one year before the publication of T. S. Eliot's *Murder in the Cathedral,* also speaks of Symons' dramas with high praise. She maintains that he is one of the few writers of the day who can write poetic dramas which are "beautiful and satisfying works of art." "He does not wish to use poetry as a means of stating his ideas about life or as a way of exploring his own mind and feelings. His emotional conflicts are stilled, his personality dimmed, so that the emotion of love and the experience of tragic events may receive their form as poetic symbols." [57]

Since Eliot's *Murder in the Cathedral* and since his theorizing on verse drama in "Poetry and Drama," however, the emphasis on "drama" has increased; action has become as important as utterance; and now one is prone to demand that "from time to time, something should happen." [58] Thouless, on the other hand, insists that the writer of poetic drama "wishes to cut away from us our own familiar world, to deprive us of the pleasure of seeing a replica of it on the stage, so that he may rouse in us unfamiliar associations, which will serve to detach the individual from his fellows, and make us feel in him the flow of inner life." [59] Thus, judging from Thouless' criteria there is something to be said for Symons' verse dramas; but, if they were performed in a theater, it is difficult to see how they could be other than dull. Compared to Eliot's exercises in the genre, they are sterile, cold, and rather pretentious.[60]

Even *The Harvesters*,[61] probably the best drama Symons wrote, is tedious and verbose. In this play we are introduced to

Michael Raven, a stern, Nonconformist Cornishman, whose daughter has been causing gossip in the village by her indiscreet behavior with her lover, Peter Corin. Unfortunately, the rumors are too well-founded; Mary becomes pregnant; and, although there is some talk of Peter's marrying her, he finally refuses. Mary then murders Peter, is brought to trial but pardoned after a short sentence in prison, and returns home. On her return she is treated coolly by the villagers, is spurned by her father, and goes off into the wilds to live with the mad Vecchan, away from the society of those whose narrow, unyielding morality will not allow them to sympathize with her.

The details of the action are managed with some skill, and a number of scenes could be successful on a stage. At the beginning of Act I, for example, the exposition is well handled. A group of women are sitting around the table in Michael Raven's kitchen, drinking tea and trying to make Mary realize the foolishness of her conduct with Peter. In the middle of their conversation they are interrupted by an offstage cry from Vecchan, and then the talk shifts from Mary to the mad woman, thus suggesting that Mary's fate is somehow linked with Vecchan's, even before the action is properly under way. In Act III, when the village awaits the coach which will bring back Mary after her pardon, Symons also builds up the tension and general air of expectancy very skillfully, so that when Mary does arrive her appearance is suitably impressive.

However, for all Symons' awareness of the demands peculiar to dramatic presentation, the play depends too much on well-worn conventions—as in the character of Vecchan, the mad woman who speaks "matter and impertinency mixed"; the introduction of a small boy who unwittingly probes Michael Raven's sorrow by naïvely insisting on knowing all the details about the girl for whom the whole village is waiting; and the heavy-handed symbolism in the choice of a sickle as the murder weapon. The diction, too, falls forever into clichés and portentous sounding phrases, as in Mary's words near the end of the play:

> All the past
> Was like a thing worn out and put away
> Not to be thought of any more; I seemed
> To drift with the present time as with a tide,
> And there was no beginning and no end.

> And when I thought and tried to stop the tide
> By thinking, I was clutching at a weed
> That the tide carried, and I hardly knew
> If I were tide or seaweed or some dream
> Of sea-birds gibbering at an ashen moon.[62]

Just as the criticism of Symons' later years is a less reliable guide to the artists he is writing about than to his own personality, so these dramas are important less for their artistic value than their interest as indications of his state of mind. All the leading characters of these plays are isolated figures, to some extent victims of their environment, who insist on a behavior that is either unacceptable or unaccountable to the society in which they live. Such, of course, is Mary in *The Harvesters*, who gives birth to an illegitimate child and murders her lover; but she is nevertheless to be pitied rather than condemned.

In *The Death of Agrippina*, Symons depicts Nero, certainly not as the sensual monster of popular imagination, but as a sensitive man who sins almost against his will, impelled by forces which he cannot control.[63] In *Cleopatra in Judaea,* Cleopatra is a heroine rather than a villainess, a dignified *femme fatale,* whose morals are not as vicious as they are unconventional;[64] the Brahmin in *The Toy Cart,* who falls in love with a courtesan and barely escapes execution, is also a victim of the society in which he lives;[65] while the two main characters in *Tristran and Iseult* oppose society together and suffer tragic consequences.[66]

In other words, the tragedies of Symons' heroes and heroines are typical of his own fate; or, as Symons suggested in *Confessions,* the characters are typical of the artist as a person who "can neither be praised nor blamed for his acceptance or rejection" of society's conventions, but who suffers, nevertheless, from his inability to make the necessary "compromise." [67]

IV *Symons and the "Moderns"*

Symons' isolation during these later years is underlined by his failure to notice in his critical writings the importance of the younger generation of literary men whom, ironically, he had done so much to encourage with his *Symbolist Movement in Literature.* T. S. Eliot, Ezra Pound, and W. B. Yeats all praised Symons' criticism of the French Symbolists; and they implied that he, in large measure, was responsible for their later poetic practices.[68] Furthermore, although Joyce himself seems not to have made specific acknowledgment of his indebtedness, David Hayman and James S. Atherton have shown that Symons' remarks on Mallarmé in particular were instrumental in shaping the novelist's esthetic.[69] It is true that before 1908 Symons had written admiringly about Yeats's work, but of his subsequent development he is silent. He probably knew something of Pound's writing; for Symons, Pound, and Ford Madox Ford are listed as contributing editors to *The Two Worlds*,[70] and Symons' work appeared twice in *The Little Review*, the *avant garde* journal of the 1920's for which Ezra Pound was European editor.[71] But Symons has nothing to say of Pound either as a critic or as a literary craftsman.

He does, however, have some perceptive comments to make about Joyce. Yeats had introduced Joyce to Symons in 1902, and soon Symons was sufficiently impressed by Joyce's talents as a poet to undertake the role of literary agent for him, eventually persuading Grant Richards to publish Joyce's first volume of poetry, *Chamber Music*.[72] When this volume appeared, Symons, one of the few reviewers to notice it, greeted Joyce's appearance as a poet as the arrival of an Irish Verlaine. He suggests that the poems in *Chamber Music* have qualities similar to those of the Elizabethan and Jacobean lyrics, and he also compares them to the drawings of Whistler. He notes that "there is no substance at all in these songs, which hardly hint at a story"; and he suggests that their effect is "like a whispering clavichord that someone plays in the evening, when it is getting dark." [73] Much later, after Joyce's *Pomes Penyeach* had appeared, whose publication, Symons notes, was as a result of his wife, Rhoda's, enthusiasm for the collection, he was still ecstatic about Joyce's poetic genius, finding in these frail songs a "rare lyrical quality with touches of pure magic." [74]

Because of the affinities of the poems in *Chamber Music* and *Pomes Penyeach* with the verse of Verlaine, one feels that Symons was more impressed with Joyce the poet than with Joyce the prose-writer. Yet, in 1914, when Symons had the opportunity to read *Dubliners*, he immediately recognized Joyce's merits as a short-story writer,[75] and by the time Symons had read *The Portrait of the Artist as a Young Man* and *Ulysses*, he was willing to recognize that Joyce was a writer of major stature, one who would undoubtedly be considered as "the most complex literary problem of this generation." What seems to have impressed Symons most was the way Joyce handled words. His vocabulary, Symons wrote, "is unusually large"; and, although he uses it "recklessly," he makes use of words in a "surprisingly novel, personal manner," evidently engaged in a search after the "virginity of language." This concern, of course, had been Mallarmé's; and Symons recognizes the similarity of their aims, noting too that such a chimerical quest is fraught with dangerous pitfalls for the literary artist, for in pursuing such an ideal the writer is liable to lapse into unintelligibility. Symons had commented on this aspect of Mallarmé's work earlier, and his fear that Joyce might also become unreadable was supported by the publication of *Finnegans Wake*.[76]

Therefore, Symons does show an intelligent awareness of some of Joyce's artistic concerns, so it is not true to say that Symons was totally insensitive to the new literary movement going on around him. However, when Symons considers Joyce as a man, he is perhaps less convincing than when he discusses his qualities as a writer. Falling victim to the neurotically subjective approach which had characterized his criticism of such writers as Baudelaire, Conrad, Rossetti, Swinburne, and Hardy, Symons describes Joyce as "a curious mixture of sinister genius and uncertain talent," a man who, for Symons at least, had a fascination that was "diabolical."[77]

Comparing Joyce to Proust, Symons notes that Pater, Byron, Joyce, and himself all suffered "from that too vivid sense of humanity which is like a disease, that obsession to which every face is a challenge and every look an acceptance or a rebuff." "How is content in life possible," he asks, "to those condemned to go about like magnets, attracting or repelling every animate thing, and tormented by the restlessness which their own presence communicates to the air around them?" Such "magnetic nature is not given to man for his happiness. It leaves him at the crowd's mercy, as he ceaselessly feels the shock of every disturbance which he causes them. Driving him into a solitude for an escape, it will not let him even then escape from the thought of what in himself is so much of an epitome of humanity, for 'quiet to quick bosoms is Hell'."[78] Symons is again talking more about himself than his subject, falling victim to the same weakness which had led him to exaggerate the neurasthenic side of Conrad's genius. The result is that, though one may admire his perceptive understanding of Joyce's technique, one rejects his total view of the man and his vision.

Oddly enough, when Symons writes of Proust, a writer whom one would expect him to have appreciated more keenly than Joyce, he is even less satisfactory and certainly less enthusiastic. He notes that Proust's conception of the novel is very different from that of the Goncourts', but he does find some resemblance in Proust's "morbid sensibility, and with this something almost incalculable which seems to come from diseased nerves, which sharpens the acuteness of every sensation to an almost vanishing point in space and which causes him to see life chiefly through this medium." [79] One can readily accept this, but Symons has nothing to say of the ambivalence of Proust's vision, preferring instead to concentrate on the novelist's insight into abnormal psychology. He points out that Proust never ventured to diagnose sadism in women, as Huysmans did; but Symons does concede that he is wonderful in his "intricate analysis of a series of states of nerves, sharpened by tragic ennui." [80] Finally, assessing Proust's status in the literary hierarchy, Symons places him on the lower slopes of Parnassus because none of his characters are tragic, and because he lacked the essential characteristics of both realistic and imaginative literature. [81]

Therefore, although Symons was not wholly oblivious of new literary figures and movements, he appears only to have been able to appreciate writers who struck a responsive chord in his own morbidly sensitive nature. Perhaps the clearest indication of his failure to understand either the extent or the nature of the changes which were taking place on the literary scene is found in an article he wrote in 1921 entitled "Some Makers of Modern Verse." For Symons, modern poetry in England seems to be that of such people as Hardy, Bridges, Kipling, and W. E. Henley. Nowhere is there mention of Eliot, Pound, or Yeats; of the Imagists; of the Georgians; and of the poets of World War I.

Yet, judging by the definition of "modernity" Symons provides in his article, one could hardly have expected otherwise. He suggests that a proper definition of the word is impossible, for poetry is "eternal"; and, although one may feel disposed to agree with him, his justification for such a view is based on 1890's Impressionism and on Verlaine's somewhat outmoded distinction between "music" and "literature." "Who can define modernity?" Symons asks. In a sense Villon was "modern":

The poetry of mere literature, like the dead body, could never bleed: a real blood rises before us in some of [Villon's] lyrics, evoked by wizard's magic—the juice of flowers in which there was no juice, evoked, that is like blood or wine. Then there were perfumed words, like women's perfumes, with visible visions of tresses of twisted hair and spun silk and the delicate texture of cobwebs. And, as on this night when I hear the moan of the wind outside my door, the wind's voice made audible in the stillness of the night, this moonlight night, covered with shining stars, so some song that might set as strange a music to the wind's wail as some song as I have never read.[82]

This, for Symons, is the eternal nature of poetry or, if one likes, of "modernity." Although at one time he had been sensitive to the development of new esthetic movements and had done so much to promote them, now he himself was left behind, a victim of the tendencies he had helped to encourage. It was a sadly ironic fate for a man who had led some of the most perceptive literary minds into the twentieth century; for, while others continued along the road he had indicated, Symons himself hovered in the shadows of the *fin-de-siècle*. It is characteristic too that just before his death he was translating Francis Carco, a French poet, novelist and critic, whose appreciative essay on Verlaine appeared in 1948, three years after Symons' death, and whose love for artistic bohemia and the Paris of the 1890's was equal only to Symons'. Yet even in translating Carco, in what must have been a labor of love, Symons' powers failed him; and his manuscript was rejected for publication.[83] Fate had reserved for him one last blow, perhaps the most cruel and ironic of all, before allowing him to slip away from a world of which he had never really been a part.

It was a sad end for a man who had once been regarded as the foremost critic, translator, and prose stylist of his day; for a poet of considerable talent; for an important influence on some of the major literary figures of the twentieth century. But memories are short, and when Symons' obituary notices appeared, almost all adopted the faintly patronizing tone appropriate to literary failures.[84] He had lived too long, and his earlier successes were largely forgotten.

CHAPTER 6

Conclusion

TO say that the work of Arthur Symons has been undeservedly neglected is to invoke one of the most shopworn clichés of literary scholarship, but it is nonetheless true. Certainly he is not a great writer, and it is equally true that, after 1908, he published very little worthy of serious consideration. It is also true that, in spite of the breadth of his interests and the variety of subjects he wrote about, his range is exceedingly limited. This limitation was recognized by the reviewer of Symons' translations from Baudelaire when he pointed out in the *Times Literary Supplement* that, although Symons was ever mindful of the aspiration of all art to the condition of music, he ought to have looked further back than Pater to Plotinus, with whom the idea originated; for the Neo-Platonist had maintained that it was necessary for there to be "base clowns and indecent drunkards in perfect drama, because perfect drama was the revelation of the unity of the world, in and through its infinite variety." [1] In Symons' world there are no "base clowns" and "indecent drunkards." His is a world from which all the raw, animal elements have been excluded, and he presents instead nervous, rose-tinted shadows, who caper suggestively in a perfumed and melancholy twilight—all pale reflections of himself.

Yet, in spite of obvious limitations, Symons did achieve a few things of permanent value. A number of his graceful lyrics, such as those from *Silhouettes* and *London Nights,* have passed into the standard repertoire of Victorian poetry anthologists. Some of his criticism, particularly his *Introduction to the Study of Robert Browning* and *The Symbolist Movement in Literature,* is both perceptive and sound, and even today may be read with profit by those who seek useful introductions to the writers concerned. His translation, notably from the French, is on the whole good but, in the case of Verlaine, excellent. And in *Spiritual Adventures* his perceptive investigations into human psychology in general and into the artistic sensibility in particular compare favorably with Pater's *Imaginary Portraits,* on which they were, in fact, modeled.

Symons also deserves a place in history for having discovered, in 1899, a mass of unpublished Casanova materials, including the missing chapters four and five of the twelfth book of the *Memoirs.* Although the existence of these papers was known to a few before Symons actually set eyes on them, he was directly responsible for the translation and inclusion of the missing chapters in the complete *Memoirs* published by The Casanova Society in 1922. Therefore, Symons must be thanked for making this material available.[2]

Yet Symons' reputation must rest less on his own work or on the discovery of the Casanova papers than on the influence he exerted on others. And when one considers that Eliot, Pound, and Yeats all spoke highly of him, while Joyce also was heavily indebted to him, his importance cannot readily be underestimated. The fact that he bridged the chasm between the Victorians and some of the greatest figures of the twentieth-century literary scene is also worth remembering, for it helps us to place the 1890's more accurately in the history of the development of English literature. Symons' literary career, perhaps more clearly than that of any of his contemporaries, shows us that the artistic sensibility did not go into hibernation at the end of the nineteenth century to reawaken somewhere around the time of World War I; it was, in fact, very much alive all the time.

Perhaps the most fascinating aspect of Symons' career, however, is the way it exemplifies the archetypal Romantic pattern, particularly as it is manifest in the careers of Wordsworth and Coleridge. Both these writers sought transcendence through an imaginative contemplation of the outward forms of nature; both at one stage in their lives penetrated to that visionary ecstasy which they had been seeking; and both experienced a falling away from Paradise in their later years. Symons too followed the Promethean pattern, mounting to the heavens in an attempt to steal the sacred fire, only to be cast down and chained to the rock of insanity and the subsequent debilitation of his artistic faculties. Wordsworth and Coleridge also paid for their vision, it is true, the one being condemned to spin out the remainder of his days in the composition of pedestrian literary exercises, the other in turgid

rationalizations of the very force which had enabled him to per-
ceive the visions of his earlier poetry.

For Symons the Gods reserved a fate more cruel, a living death
of remembrance of things past without the consolation of knowing that at least he had "fed on honey-dew, and drunk the milk of
Paradise." Like Berlioz, about whom Symons had written in *The
Saturday Review,* Symons' "failure" was like the fall of Icarus; his
wings melted from him at a great height, and there was no one to
lift him after his fall. His tireless ambition carried him again and
again into the unattainable skies, and again and again he felt
under him the hardness of the inhospitable earth.[3]

Notes and References

Chapter One

1. Frank Harris, *Oscar Wilde: His Life and His Confessions* (New York, 1918), I, 49.

2. T. S. Eliot, "The Place of Pater" in *The 1880's,* ed. Walter de la Mare (Cambridge, 1930), pp. 100–05.

3. Oscar Wilde, "Mr. Pater's Last Volume," *The Speaker,* March 22, 1890, reprinted. *The Complete Works of Oscar Wilde,* ed. Robert Ross (London, 1908), IX, 538.

4. *Ibid.,* X, 26–28. See also X, 156–59.

5. Oscar Wilde, *De Profundis,* ed. Vyvyan Holland (New York, 1950), p. 85.

6. See Geoffrey Tillotson, *Criticism and the Nineteenth Century* (London, 1951), p. 137. Tillotson suggests that the fault was not entirely Wilde's, but Pater's, whose Conclusion lays itself open to misinterpretation. On the other hand Graham Hough blames Wilde: "Wilde's aestheticism was little more than a series of attitudes and undigested notions, held together for a time by what have been a brilliant and attractive personality." *The Last Romantics* (London: 1949), p. 203.

7. Walter Pater, *The Renaissance* (New York, 1913), pp. 236–38.

8. See Graham Hough, *The Last Romantics,* p. 140.

9. Walter Pater, *The Renaissance,* p. 239.

10. See Frank Kermode, *Romantic Images* (London, 1957), p. 20.

11. Oscar Wilde, *Complete Works,* X, 28.

12. Walter Pater, *Uncollected Essays* (Portland, Maine, 1903), p. 127.

13. Walter Pater, *The Renaissance,* p. 233n. See J. H. Buckley, "Pater and the Suppressed 'Conclusion'," LXV *Modern Language Notes* (1950), 249–51.

14. E. K. Brown, "Pater's *Appreciations:* A Bibliographical Note," *Ibid.,* LXV (1950), 247–49.

15. Symons received his first letter from Pater in 1886, acknowledging the receipt of *An Introduction to the Study of Robert Browning,* but the two men did not meet until two years later. See Arthur Symons,

"Some Browning Reminiscences," *North American Review,* CCIV (1916), 602–03.

16. Symons described his early years in "A Prelude to Life" in *Spiritual Adventures* (London, 1906), pp. 3–54. For a fuller account see Roger Lhombreaud, *Arthur Symons* (London, 1963), pp. 3–57. Lhombreaud reprints a few lines from "A Dream of the Garden of God," a rather pedestrian piece of Tennysonian sanctimoniousness, and notes that the original MS in the Houghton Library, Harvard University, bears the inscription in his mother's handwriting: "written by Symons at the age of 13" (9, 310). Although Symons rebelled when still quite young, against the pious restrictions of his Methodist upbringing, it is perhaps worth noting that in his early publications he frequently assumes the role of the religious moralist. In his first major publication, for example, a facsimile edition of the *Venus and Adonis* quarto, he regrets that there are passages in Shakespeare's poem which on moral grounds are inexcusable. However, he suggests that Shakespeare redeems himself by his *"moral reflectiveness,* which we seek in vain to find in Ovid, together with an 'outdoor poetry,' which is purely English and entirely admirable." Therefore, "the important thing to note is, that a *sense of moral fitness* being here present, though only as an adjunct or appendage, and by no means a guiding principle, this quality, strengthened with the experience and the growing calmness of years, may in time become a guiding principle." Arthur Symons, "Introduction," *Venus and Adonis,* Shakespeare Quarto Facsimiles, XII (London, 1885), p. xvi.

17. Arthur Symons, *Spiritual Adventures,* p. 34.

18. Graham Hough, *The Last Romantics,* p. 166.

19. Roger Lhombreaud, *Arthur Symons,* p. 10.

20. "Introduction," *Venus and Adonis,* p. xix.

21. "Introduction," *The Best Plays of Philip Massinger,* Mermaid Series (London: 1887), p. xv.

22. "Introduction," *Leigh Hunt's Essays* (London, 1888), p. xvii. In the notes to this volume Symons also suggests that Hunt's "The Fair Revenge" has something of the "quiet charm of narrative" reminiscent of "Dennys l'Auxerrois" and "Sebastian Van Storck," two of Pater's *Imaginary Portraits.*

23. "Introduction," *Nero and Other Plays,* Mermaid Series (London, 1886), pp. 200–01.

24. See, however, "Credo," p. 41.

25. "Walter Pater," in *Studies in Prose and Verse* (London, 1904), p. 63.

26. *Ibid.,* pp. 64–65.

21. *Ibid.,* p. 65

28. *Ibid.,* p. 73.

29. *Ibid.*, p. 74.

30. *Figures of Several Centuries* (London, 1916), p. 322.

31. Roger Lhombreaud, *Arthur Symons*, p. 23.

32. One of the more interesting papers which Symons read was on Browning's qualities as a dramatist, "Is Browning Dramatic?" which he delivered at the twenty-ninth meeting of The Browning Society, January 30, 1885 (Vol. II, No. 4). He insists that Browning is dramatic, but not in the Shakespearian sense; for Browning is more concerned with what Symons calls "a drama of the interior, a tragedy or comedy of the soul." This, evidently, was also Symons' aim in his first published volume of poems, *Days and Nights*.

33. *Figures of Several Centuries*, p. 354. There is a sympathetic portrait of James Dykes Campbell in Symons' "Some Browning Reminiscences," *North American Review*, CCIV (1916), 602–09. Campbell was responsible for introducing Symons to Browning, shortly after his study of the poet had appeared. It was the only time Symons met Browning personally.

34. *An Introduction to the Study of Robert Browning*, new edn. revised and enlarged (London, 1906), p. 23. I have referred to this later edition as it is more accessible than the earlier. In none of the passages referred to is there any change from the 1886 version.

35. *Ibid.*, p. 129.

36. *Ibid.*, pp. 9–10.

31. Pater himself had suggested the relationship between his own esthetic and Browning's in his essay on Winckelmann in *The Renaissance*, from which Symons' quotation is taken. Symons has merely suppressed Pater's overt references to Browning, replacing them with ellipses. Pater also reviewed favorably Symons' study of Browning in *The Guardian*. Walter Pater, *Essays from the Guardian* (London, 1913), pp. 42–51.

38. Although *Days and Nights* was Symons' first volume of poems to be published, it by no means represents the greater part of his early output. As early as 1879 there existed a MS volume of poems written at Tiverton, and in 1880 there were two more, one written at Tiverton and Bideford, and the third at Bideford. Allen Wade, "Arthur Symons," *Times Literary Supplement*, March 10, 1945, p. 115.

39. *Collected Works* (London, 1924), I, 3–5. See also *An Introduction to the Study of Robert Browning*, p. 27.

40. *Collected Works*, I, 61–67. T. Earle Welby writes: "Only the fact that Wilde's boyish melodrama, 'Vera', was then unpublished holds me from suspecting that it had something to do with the origin of 'An Episode Under the Nihilists'." T. Earle Welby, *Arthur Symons* (London, 1924), p. 20. On the contrary, *Vera* had been published, first in London in 1880; and two years later a privately printed edition came

out in New York. However, both editions are exceedingly rare. See
Stuart Mason, *Bibliography of Oscar Wilde* (London, 1939), pp. 249–
281.

41. *Collected Works*, I, 43–46.

42. *Ibid.*, I, 83.

43. *Ibid.*, I, 12–13. Cf. R. L. Stevenson's "The Sick Child" in *Underwoods, Collected Works* (New York, 1889), XV, 50–51.

44. *Collected Works*, I, 6–8, 9–11, 36–37. Many years after the
publication of *Days and Nights* Symons noted that *Les Fleurs du Mal*
"was at once a fascination and an influence" in regard to his earliest
verses, Arthur Symons, *Baudelaire: Prose and Poetry* (New York,
1926), pp. v-viii. It seems unlikely that he was referring to *Days and
Nights* when he made this statement, as Baudelaire's influence is not
especially apparent in this volume. What Symons probably had in mind
were those verses which though written in his youth, were not published until much later. See *Lesbia and Other Poems*.

45. Walter Pater, *Sketches and Reviews*, ed. A. Mordell (New York,
1913), p. 135.

46. *Ibid.*, p. 134.

47. *Ibid.*, pp. 140–41. Symons had written to Pater before the publication of *Days and Nights*, enclosing two Browningesque poems, "Bell
in Camp" and "A Revenge," requesting the master's comments. Pater
replied on January 8, 1888, assuring Symons that he had "a poetic
talent remarkable, especially at the present day, for precise and intellectual grasp on the matter it deals with," and praising "A Revenge,"
which he greatly preferred to "Bell in Camp." Nevertheless, in spite
of his affirmation of Symons' poetic talent, he suggests that Symons turn
his attention to prose "and publish [his] verse as an intimate gift for
those who already value [him] for [his] pedestrian work in literature,"
because he thinks the present age unfavorable for poets. Symons published Pater's letter in full in "Walter Pater" in *Figures of Several Centuries*, pp. 325–26.

48. *Collected Works*, I, 50–53.

49. *Spiritual Adventures*, p. 37.

50. *Ibid.*, p. 38.

51. *Collected Works*, I, 86.

52. *Ibid.*, I, 92.

Chapter Two

1. T. Earle Welby, *Arthur Symons*, p. 15. See also Roger Lhombreaud, *Arthur Symons*, pp. 34–35.

2. Havelock Ellis, *From Rousseau to Proust* (Boston, 1935), pp. 4–5.

3. *Ibid.*, pp. 6–11.

4. Edmund Wilson, *Axel's Castle* (New York, 1931), p. 19.

5. *Ibid.*, p. 21.

6. C. M. Bowra, *The Heritage of Symbolism* (London, 1943), p. 9.

7. A. G. Lehmann, *The Symbolist Aesthetic in France: 1885–1895* (Oxford, 1950), pp. 149 ff.

8. C. M. Bowra, *The Heritage of Symbolism*, p. 11.

9. *Ibid.*, p. 2.

10. *Ibid.*, p. 3.

11. George Moore, *Confessions of a Young Man*, 2nd edn. (London, 1904), p. 62.

12. George Moore, *Impressions and Opinions* (London, 1891), pp. 114–15.

13. Edmund Gosse, *Questions at Issue* (London, 1893), p. 226.

14. Edmund Gosse, "Current French Literature," *Cosmopolis*, II (June, 1896), 674.

15. "Review of 'Bonheur'," *Academy*, XXXIX (April 18, 1891), 362.

16. "Paul Verlaine," *National Review*, XIX (June, 1892), 501–15.

17. "The Decadent Movement in Literature", *Harper's New Monthly Magazine*, LXXXVII (November, 1893), 858–67.

18. Arthur Symons, *Mes Souvenirs* (Eure, France, 1930), p. 3.

19. Richard Le Gallienne, *Retrospective Reviews* (London, 1896), I, 24–26.

20. "The Decadent Movement in Literature," p. 859.

21. *Ibid.*, p. 858.

22. *Collected Works*, I, 197.

23. *Ibid.*, I, 206. At a later date Symons described the genesis of this poem in an unpublished MS entitled "Sensations." He refers to "Dawn" as one of his favorite pieces, noting that it was prompted by an evening spent with a young prostitute on January 12, 1892, whom he had met on the promenade at The Empire Music-Hall. Judging by his later description of the event, Symons was perhaps a little less philosophical concerning the bitter-sweetness of his relationship with the young woman than he appears to have been in the published poem: "She was one of the youngest and of the most beautiful girls I have ever met. Her youth, her rare beauty, her amazing and absolute innocence, her delicious sense of surprise . . . and that joy of life which was part of the freshness and the fairness of youth: all that, which was not exactly new to me, instilled into my very blood a sense of pity which I had never felt before in all my intercourse with harlots."

He goes on to describe her appearance in particularly frank detail, dwelling at length on her way of undressing and his reaction to her youthful coyness. As Symons relives the emotions of the event, he reveals some of the senile pruriency which discolors much of his later writing, making it difficult for us to accept his statement that there is considerable "purity" in his descriptions of relationships with women: "I sometimes think, that in many of my poems on the subject of harlots, I have given evidence of the purity of my intentions, apart from the supposed or imaginary impurity of such subjects as these. One requires in such verses the simple sudden sound of plain lines which should show, at least, one's absolute poetic power upon words." Arthur Symons, "My Planets," unpublished MS in the Symons Collection at Princeton University, n.d.

24. Charles Morice, *La Littérature de tout à l'heure* (Paris, 1889), p. 198.

25. See *The Autobiography of W. B. Yeats* (New York: 1954), p. 202.

26. "The Decadent Movement in Literature," p. 862.

27. *Ibid.* (Cf. Charles Morice, *La littérature de tout à l'heure,* p. 281.)

28. *Ibid.*

29. *Ibid.,* p. 859.

30. *Ibid.,* p. 866.

31. *Ibid.,* p. 864.

32. *Ibid.,* p. 867.

33. "The Decadent Movement in Literature" in *Dramatis Personae* (Indianapolis: 1923).

34. *Figures of Several Centuries* (London, 1916), p. 127.

35. *Studies in Two Literatures* (London, 1897), p. 79.

36. *Ibid.,* p. 291.

37. *Ibid.,* p. 237.

38. *Ibid.,* pp. 239–40.

39. *Ibid.,* p. 232.

40. *Ibid.,* p. 271.

41. *Ibid.,* p. 297.

42. *Ibid.,* p. 298.

43. *Ibid.,* pp. 298–99.

44. Symons himself in a number of unpublished autobiographical fragments now in the Symons Collection at Princeton University described his amatory exercises in some detail. See for example "My Planets," parts of which are quoted on pp. 143–44. In some of his later published writings Symons also is far from reticent. See for example his preface to *Manon Lescaut,* trans. D. C. Moylan, illus. by Allastair (London, 1928), p. x and *Mes Souvenirs,* pp. 33–37.

45. On one occasion John Addington Symonds, Ernest Dowson, and some of Symons' lady friends from the ballet all tried hashish during an afternoon tea given by Symons in his rooms at Fountain Court. In describing the affair Symons again gives evidence of detachment

from his surroundings, making it seem that his responsibility for stage-managing the event gave him as much pleasure as the social occasion itself:

On the following afternoon Dowson turned up, then the ballet-girls one after another, whose laughter and whose youth always enchanted me; then Symonds, whose entrance seemed to disturb them; they began to be curiously nervous and he by being for a few minutes nervously shy. Yet when, with the gravity of a Doge, he handed round the tea, and I the cakes and cigarettes, we suddenly became quite at home. Later on we tried the effect haschisch—that slow intoxication, that elaborate experiment in visionary sensations, which to Dowson at Oxford had been his favourite form of intoxication, which, however, had no effect on him, as he sat, a little anxiously, with, as his habit was, his chin on his breast, awaiting the magic, half shy in the midst of that bright company of young people, of which I was the host and the gatherer, whom he had seen only across the footlights.

"John Addington Symonds," unpublished MS in the Symons Collection, Princeton University Library, n.d.

46. William Rothenstein once remarked that Symons was "a veritable amateur of artists, and collected them with the passion others have for china and pictures, poring over his impressions of their characters like a connoisseur over his treasures." *Men and Memories* (New York, 1932), II, 47.

47. *Parisian Nights* (London, 1926), pp. 10–13.

48. After his first trip abroad in 1889 Symons returned to the Continent many times, travelling as far as Moscow during the summer of 1897. Later, accompanied by his wife, he visited the Baltic countries and Turkey.

49. During the early years of the 1890's when Symons was music-hall critic for *The Star*, he published his impressions of music-hall entertainment in England, France and Spain.

50. Many of these notebooks have been preserved in the Symons Collection at Princeton University Library. Particularly interesting in relation to the above is a small, black notebook in which Symons jotted down his impressions of a number of Parisian music-halls and circuses which he visited during May, 1892.

51. *Colour Studies in Paris* (New York, 1918), p. 118.

52. *Collected Works*, I, 119.

53. *Ibid.*, I, 124.

54. *Ibid.*, I, 269.

55. William Rothenstein, *Men and Memories*, I, 148.

56. Paul Verlaine, trans. Arthur Symons, "My Visit to London," *The Savoy*, II (April, 1896), 120–21.

57. Arthur Waugh (1866–1943), for many years associated with the publishing house of Chapman and Hall, and author of an article attacking his contemporaries for lack of modesty in their writings ("Reticence in Literature," *The Yellow Book*, I [April, 1894], 201–19.), described the occasion with these words: "The reading of the liturgical odes in his religious volume called *Sagesse*, caused a positive thrill to pass through the audience . . . and many must have doubted whether the *vox humana* notes was ever more penetratingly employed." "London Letter," *The Critic*, December 9, 1893, p. 383.

The two lady poets who went under the collective name of "Michael Field" were also present at this reading, and they too recorded their favorable impressions of the event. See *Works and Days*, ed. T. and D. C. Sturge Moore, November 22, 1893 (London, 1933), pp. 188–189.

58. Oliver Elton, *Frederick York Powell* (Oxford, 1906), I, 153–54.

59. Georges Jean-Aubry, "Paul Verlaine et l'Angleterre: 1872–1892," *Revue de Paris*, VI (December 1, 1918), 600–20.

60. V. P. Underwood, *Verlaine et l'Angleterre* (Paris, 1956), pp. 470–71.

61. Paul Verlaine, *Oeuvres Posthûmes*, III, 188, quoted V. P. Underwood, *Verlaine et l'Angleterre*, p. 472.

62. "Mr. Henley's Poetry," *Fortnightly Review*, LII (August, 1892), 185.

63. "Paul Verlaine," *National Review*, XIX (June, 1892), 502. Moore was considerably less charitable about Verlaine's appearance, drawing attention to the poet's "bold, prominent forehead (une tête glabre), the cavernous eyes," and the "macabre expression of burnt-out lust on his face." *Impressions and Opinions*, p. 101. See also George Moore, *Memories of My Dead Life* (London, 1906), p. 80, and his *Conversations in Ebury Street* (London, 1930), p. 104. It was said, too, that Oscar Wilde found Verlaine's appearance so objectionable that he refused to meet him a second time. Hesketh Pearson, *Oscar Wilde: His Life and Wit* (New York, 1946), p. 72.

64. *Colour Studies in Paris*, p. 224.

65. "A Literary Causerie: On the Invectives of Verlaine," *The Savoy*, VII (November, 1896), 88–90.

66. "Paul Verlaine," *National Review*, XIX (June, 1892), 515. (See also Ruth Temple, *Critic's Alchemy*, p. 144.)

67. *Ibid.*

68. "Review of 'Bonheur'," *Academy*, XXXIX (April 18, 1891), 362.

69. *The Symbolist Movement in Literature* ed. Richard Ellmann (New York: 1958), p. 48.

70. *Collected Works*, I, 134.

71. "Should Translators Improve Their Authors?", *Bookman Journal*, V (January, 1922), 109–12.

72. Appendix to *The Symbolist Movement in Literature* (London, 1908). Although Symons did not complete this project, most of his translations from Verlaine's poems, including "Cortège," appeared in a later collection of verse, *Knave of Hearts* (1913). See Arthur Symons, *Collected Works*, III, 83–168.

73. Harold Nicolson, *Paul Verlaine* (London, 1921), p. 241.

74. "Review of 'Bonheur,' " p. 362.

75. *Collected Works*, I, 216.

76. *Ibid.*, I, 96–97.

77. The poet William Watson, particularly outraged by Beardsley's contributions to *The Yellow Book*, presented an ultimatum to the publishers that either Beardsley would have to go or he would refuse to submit any more material for publication in the magazine. Beardsley "resigned" from his position as art editor with the fifth issue, and all the designs he had made for this number were cancelled, the work of other artists being substituted instead. For a detailed account of the charges of immorality and of Beardsley's departure from *The Yellow Book* see Katherine Lyon Mix, *A Study in Yellow* (Lawrence, Kansas, 1960), pp. 140–52.

78. *Ibid.*, p. 160.

79. For a brief description of the origins of *The Savoy* see E. Lenore Casford, *The Magazines of the 1890's*, University of Oregon Publications, Language and Literature Series, I (September, 1929), 20. See also Arthur Symons, "A Literary Causerie: By Way of Epilogue," *The Savoy*, VIII (December, 1896), 92.

80. "Editorial Note," *The Savoy*, I (January, 1896), 5.

81. "A Literary Causerie: By Way of Epilogue," p. 91.

82. Anon., *Punch*, February 1, 1896, p. 49. Casford quotes this passage as indicative of *Punch's* approval of the magazine. Evidently she consulted only the press notices which Symons included in the final pages of the second number (see *The Savoy*, II, April, 1896, 203). Reference to the original, as might be expected, makes clear *Punch's* ironical intentions, and it seems that Symons in quoting this passage was either deliberately misleading his public, or more probably, sharing a joke with his readers.

83. *Academy*, XLIX (January 18, 1896), 56.

84. *The Athenaeum*, January 28, 1896, p. 117.

85. Quoted Joseph Hone, *W. B. Yeats* (New York, 1943), p. 130.

86. Quoted A. N. Jeffares, *W. B. Yeats: Man and Poet* (New Haven, 1949), p. 104.

87. See Katherine Lyon Mix, *A Study in Yellow*, p. 204.

88. Arthur Symons, "At the Alhambra," *The Savoy*, V (September, 1896), 75.

89. *Ibid.*, pp. 76–80.

90. Thomas Jay Garbaty, "The French Côterie of *The Savoy* 1896," *PMLA*, LXXV (1960), 609–15.

91. That *Le Centaur* was directly modeled on *The Savoy* is substantiated by Ernest Dowson in a letter to Arthur Symons. See John M. Munro, "A Previously Unpublished Letter from Ernest Dowson to Arthur Symons," *Etudes Anglaises*, XVII, 3 (July-September, 1964), 284–87.

92. Richard Le Gallienne, "To the Reader" in *English Poems* (London, 1894).

93. Richard Le Gallienne, "Review of *Silhouettes*," *Retrospective Reviews* (London, 1896), I, 181.

94. *Dramatis Personae* (Indianapolis, 1923), p. 133.

95. *Collected Works*, I, 107.

96. *Ibid.*, I, 126.

97. *Ibid.*, I, 145.

98. *Ibid.*, I, 170.

99. *Ibid.*, I, 282.

100. *Ibid.*, I, 330–31.

101. Paul Elmer More, "Arthur Symons: The Two Illusions" in *Shelburne Essays*, First Series (Boston, 1907), p. 143.

102. William Archer, *Poets of the Younger Generation* (New York, 1902), p. 412.

103. "Confessions," *The Two Worlds*, II, 5 (September, 1926), 27–34.

104. None of these later poems about Lydia have any artistic value, but they do provide dramatic evidence of the lasting impression she made upon her lover. The following, written in 1940 when Symons was in his seventies, is preserved among the Symons papers at Princeton:

Lydia

Passion was secret to the Universe,
That is, the Universe we both lived in.
Our eyes, our Guilty Gates, let out some Sin,
And that the Soul had hidden. What Primeval Curse
Had been thrown upon us? What could be worse
Than that? Seven Devils in a dusy [busy?] Inn,
Who being naked showed all their Skin,
And who danced before the Whirling Univ

> And then I prayed that Jesus Christ, Our Lord,
> For Lydia's sake and mine. Now what girl at her age
> Could be seductive before she was adored?
> She was a Perfect Dancer on the Stage.
> Both guilty, she left me at the Guilty Ford,
> And that was the end of our Passionate Pilgrimage.

105. *Spiritual Adventures,* pp. 23–24.
106. *Collected Works,* III, 61.
107. "Paul Verlaine," *National Review,* XIX (June, 1892), 503.

Chapter Three

1. Richard Ellmann, *Yeats: The Man and the Masks,* p. 25.
2. *Ibid.,* pp. 41–67.
3. *Ibid.,* p. 86.
4. W. B. Yeats, *A Vision,* 2nd edn. (New York, 1938), p. 72.
5. Virginia Moore, *The Unicorn* (New York, 1954), p. 85.
6. *The Letters of W. B. Yeats,* ed. Allan Wade (London, 1954), p. 167.
7. *The Autobiography of W. B. Yeats* (New York, 1953), p. 191.
8. Quoted A. N. Jeffares in *W. B. Yeats: Man and Poet,* p. 99.
9. *The Autobiography of W. B. Yeats,* p. 184. For a more detailed statement concerning Johnson's distaste for Symons' poetry see p. 116.
10. *Ibid.,* p. 191.
11. *Ibid.* Yeats also expressed his admiration of the Rhymers in "The Grey Rock," *Collected Poems* (London, 1955), pp. 115–19.
12. Quoted Richard Ellmann, *Yeats: The Man and the Masks,* p. 141.
13. *The Autobiography of W. B. Yeats,* p. 102.
14. Quoted Richard Ellmann, *Yeats: The Man and the Masks,* p. 141.
15. W. B. Yeats, "A Symbolical Drama in Paris," *The Bookman,* VI (April–September, 1894), 14–16.
16. Symons had moved into Fountain Court in February, 1891, remaining there until he married Rhoda Bowser in 1901. Yeats has an amusing account of his and Symons' understanding in connection with their receiving guests at Fountain Court. Apparently they had rooms next to each other, and Yeats's "opened through a little passage into those of Arthur Symons. If anybody rang at either door one or the other would look through a window in the connecting passage and report. [They] would then decide whether one or both should receive the visitor, whether [Symons'] door or [Yeats's] should be opened, or whether both doors were to remain closed." *The Autobiography of W. B. Yeats,* p. 194.

17. *Ibid.*, p. 192.

18. *Ibid.*, p. 119.

19. *Ibid.*, pp. 201–02.

20. W. B. Yeats, *Essays and Introductions* (New York, 1961), p. 150.

21. Although *The Symbolist Movement in Literature* bears 1899 as its publication date, it actually appeared in 1900, a delay evidently occasioned by the Boer War. See Roger Lhombreaud, *Arthur Symons,* p. 166.

22. Ruth Z. Temple in her criticism of *The Symbolist Movement in Literature* is particularly flattering, singling out the essays on Verlaine, Mallarmé, and Laforgue for special commendation, but suggesting also that the essay on Rimbaud is poor, giving the impression that Symons knew Rimbaud only at second hand (*The Critic's Alchemy,* pp. 153–173). On the other hand, Bruce Morisette has said that "not one of Symons' essays is regarded by any present-day critic as a valid presentation of the doctrine or technique of the poet with whom it deals." "Early English and American Critics of French Symbolism" in *Studies in Honor of Frederick W. Shipley* (St. Louis, Mo., 1942), p. 166. *The Symbolist Movement in Literature* also suffered from extensive revision. The first edition is dated 1899, but a second edition appeared in 1908, substantially the same as the first except that the essay on Huysmans was revised and brought up to date. However, when a third edition came out in 1919, the character of the book had changed considerably because included were essays on Baudelaire, who has some claim to be considered as a Symbolist, and also pieces on such unrelated figures as Balzac, Prosper Merimée, Flaubert, the brothers Goncourt, Léon Cladel and Zola. Furthermore, almost as if Symons had attempted to destroy all notions that these writers ever belonged to a movement, the complimentary dedication to W. B. Yeats was omitted. Finally, in his *Collected Works* the title *Symbolist Movement in Literature* disappears altogether, some studies of English writers are added, and the new volume is given the name of a book Symons had published in 1897, *Studies in Two Literatures.*

23. *Collected Works,* I, 166.

24. *Ibid.,* I, 165.

25. *Collected Works,* I, 166. Cf. Yeats's essay, "The Moods," in *Essays and Introductions,* pp. 195–96.

26. "From a Castle in Ireland," *The Savoy,* VI (October, 1896), 95. It should be mentioned, however, that in the next issue of the magazine Symons refers to the publication of his forthcoming volume called *The Decadent Movement in Literature,* which was to contain essays on "Joris-Karl Huysmans, Paul Verlaine, the Goncourts, Villiers de l'Isle Adam and Maurice Maeterlinck." *The Savoy,* VIII (December,

1896), 95. Evidently at this time the new epithet "Symbolist" had not been decided upon.

27. *The Autobiography of W. B. Yeats,* pp. 223–24.

28. *Collected Works,* II, 336.

29. Roger Lhombreaud, *Arthur Symons,* p. 135.

30. *The Symbolist Movement in Literature,* pp. xx. Symons expects his readers to be surprised at finding him, of all people, writing about the spirit world. Yet progress towards such an attitude was by no means uncommon among Symons' contemporaries in the 1890's. Towards the end of their lives, Wilde and Beardsley both turned to the Roman Catholic Church, hoping to find there the security and peace that had eluded them for so long; and John Gray and Ernest Dowson were also converted at earlier stages of their careers.

Indeed, far from being an isolated phenomenon, this yearning for the spirit-world has been characterized by Mario Praz as a conventional Decadent concern (see *The Romantic Agony, passim*). Praz sees it as a retreat into the world of dreams, an escape from a life of action; and no doubt to many of Symons' contemporaries this is precisely what it was. To Symons, however, it was not so much a withdrawal as an advance, for his earlier pursuit of hedonistic pleasure had brought him disillusionment, and his desire to transcend the circumstances of this world was an attempt to find a more meaningful solution to the problem of existence.

31. *The Symbolist Movement in Literature,* pp. 4–5. Symons had previously put forward the idea that "decadence" should only be applied to style in an essay on Meredith: "What Decadence, in literature, really means, is that learned corruption of language by which style ceases to be organic, and becomes, in this pursuit of some new expressiveness or beauty, deliberately normal." Arthur Symons, *Studies in Prose and Verse,* p. 149.

A similar conclusion concerning the meaning of the word "decadence" had been reached by Symons' friend Havelock Ellis at approximately the same time: "Technically a decadent style is only such in relation to a classic style, a further specialisation, the homogeneous, in Spencerean phraseology, having become heterogeneous. The first is beautiful because the parts are subordinated to the whole, the second is beautiful because the whole is subordinate to the parts." Havelock Ellis, *Affirmations* (London, 1898), p. 175.

32. W. B. Yeats, *Essays and Introductions,* pp. 193–94.

33. *The Letters of W. B. Yeats,* p. 337.

34. *The Symbolist Movement in Literature,* p. 12.

35. *Ibid.,* p. 74.

36. *Ibid.,* p. 84.

37. *Ibid.,* p. 48.

38. *Ibid.,* p. 39.

39. *Ibid.,* p. 32.

40. *Ibid.,* p. 80.

41. *Ibid.,* p. xiii.

42. *Ibid.,* pp. 95–96.

43. W. B. Yeats, *Essays and Introductions,* pp. 163–64.

44. *Ibid.,* p. 161.

45. *The Symbolist Movement in Literature,* pp. 70–71.

46. *Ibid.,* p. 69.

47. Ruth Z. Temple, *The Critic's Alchemy,* p. 165.

48. *The Symbolist Movement in Literature,* pp. 71–72.

49. *Studies in Prose and Verse,* p. 231. Later in this essay Symons is more explicit in his recognition of Yeats's esthetic intentions, describing the poet's verse with words that recall Yeats's essay on the "new" poetry in "The Autumn of the Body": "Here, at last, is poetry which has found for itself a new form, a form really modern, in its rejection of every artifice, its return to the natural chant out of which verse was evolved, and it expresses, with a passionate quietude, the elemental desires of humanity, the desire of love, the desire of wisdom, the desire of beauty" (p. 235).

50. *Collected Works,* II, 36–40.

51. *Ibid.,* II, 62–63, 70–71, 108.

52. *Ibid.,* II, 109.

53. See, for example, *Ibid.,* II, 127–28, 135, 136, 140, 141, 147, all of which reveal the unmistakable influence of Donne.

54. Gabriele d'Annunzio, *The Child of Pleasure,* trans. Georgina Hardy, verses trans. and intro. by Arthur Symons (New York, 1898), p. vi.

55. *Studies in Prose and Verse,* pp. 126–28.

56. Arthur Symons, Ed. *The Poems of Ernest Dowson* (London, 1914), pp. xviii–xx. At this time Symons also recognized the "Symbolist" qualities in the work of another of his so-called Decadent contemporaries, Aubrey Beardsley. He points out that there is nothing "animal" about his designs, there being instead "a sort of abstract spiritual corruption, revealed in beautiful form; sin transfigured by beauty. And here, even if we go no further, is an art intensely spiritual, an art in which evil purifies itself by its own intensity, and by the beauty which transfigures it . . . it is the triumph of the spirit over the flesh, to no matter what end. It is a form of divine possession, by which the inactive and materialising soul is set in fiery motion, lured from the ground, into at least a certain high liberty." *Aubrey Beardsley* (London, 1948), p. 21.

57. *Figures of Several Centuries,* pp. 10–12.

58. *Ibid.,* pp. 91–100. See also Symons' essay on "Welsh Poetry,"

in which he notes its dependence on "precise images" through which the Celtic bards "approached the unseen." *Ibid.*, p. 393.

59. *The Autobiography of W. B. Yeats*, p. 119. See p. 78.

60. W. B. Yeats, "The Rhymers' Club" in *Letters to the New Island* (Cambridge, Mass., 1934), p. 144.

61. William Rothenstein, *Men and Memories*, I, 239.

62. Arthur Symons, *Cities, Seacoasts and Islands* (New York, 1919), pp. 204–05. Previously published in *London: A Book of Aspects*, privately printed, 1909.

63. *Colour Studies in Paris*, pp. 107–18.

64. *Collected Works*, I, 125. This poem later appeared in *The Book of the Rhymers' Club* (London, 1892), p. 57, where the last three lines were changed to: "The little amber-colored dancers move,/ Like little painted figures on a screen,/ Among the shadows of a magic grove."

65. See John M. Munro, "Arthur Symons, 'The Symphony of Snakes,' and the Development of the Romantic Image," *English Literature in Transition*, VII, 3 (1964), 143–45, and Edward Baugh's reply in the next issue of the same journal, VII, 4 (1964), 228–29.

66. *Collected Works*, I, 305.

67. Quoted Richard Ellmann, *The Identity of Yeats* (New York, 1954), pp. 166–67.

68. *Studies in Seven Arts*, pp. 387–91.

69. *The Autobiography of W. B. Yeats*, pp. 191–92.

70. Frank Kermode, *Romantic Image*, p. 68. "At the Ball" in *Collected Works*, I, 59; "In the Haymarket," I, 120; "Javanese Dancers," I, 125. See also W. B. Yeats, "The Man Who Dreamed of Fairyland" in *Collected Poems*, p. 50.

71. W. B. Yeats, "Rosa Alchemica," *The Savoy*, II (April, 1896), 56–70.

72. For a good discussion of the image of the dance in both Symons and Yeats, see Ian Fletcher, "Explorations and Recoveries II," *The London Magazine*, VII, 6 (June, 1960), 49–60.

73. Richard Ellmann, "Introduction," *The Symbolist Movement in Literature*, p. xi. That Yeats was a major influence on Symons' development as a writer is supported by a letter from Rhoda Symons to the poet in 1908, informing him of her husband's condition:

Though of late years Arthur greatly regretted not seeing you more often, you were the man nearest to him. The one he honoured & admired most. His mind has given way. It happened in Italy. I sent two male nurses to bring him home. Rizian [?] Russell, the best man in London saw him yesterday. He says it is general paralysis. There is no hope—he will not let me keep him at home & indeed it is im-

possible, he wants to lock me into a room with him. So today we take
him to a private doctor's home, where he will be extremely well looked
after. I feel stunned & quite incapable of doing anything—he has
devoured your collected edition which he found on his return—mur-
muring "beautiful—beautiful"—it is terrible—perhaps sometime you
will go & see him at Crowborough—it would be more than a kindness
on your part.

Yours gratefully for all
you have been to him—
Rhoda Symons

A. L. S., Berg Collection, New York Public Library, Folder 64B8375.
    74. Max Beerbohm, *Works and More* (London, 1952), pp. 115–24.
    75. *The Symbolist Movement in Literature,* p. xx.
    76. Richard Ellmann, "Introduction," *The Symbolist Movement in Literature,* p. xiv.
    77. *Collected Works,* II, 3–25.
    78. *Ibid.,* II, 127.
    79. *Ibid.,* II, 140.

Chapter Four

1. *Plays, Acting and Music,* pp. vii–ix.
2. *Figures of Several Centuries,* pp. 320–21.
3. *Ibid.,* p 318.
4. *Studies in Seven Arts,* p. 301.
5. *Ibid.,* p. 302.
6. *Ibid.,* p. 303.
7. *The Symbolist Movement in Literature,* p. 71.
8. W. B. Yeats, *Essays and Introductions,* pp. 156–57.
9. See p. 77.
10. *Plays, Acting and Music,* pp. 7–8.
11. *Ibid.,* p. 8.
12. *Ibid.,* pp. 52–53.
13. *Ibid.,* p. 59.
14. *Ibid.,* p. 28.
15. *Ibid.,* p. 38.
16. *Ibid.,* p. 61.
17. *Ibid.,* pp. 167–72.
18. *Ibid., pp.* 162–65.
19. *Studies in Seven Arts,* pp. 349–60.
20. *Ibid.,* pp. 365–66.
21. *Plays, Acting and Music,* pp. 321–22.
22. "Pachmann and Paderewski," *Saturday Review,* CVI (July 25, 1908), 110.

23. *Plays, Acting and Music,* p. 269.
24. *Studies in Seven Arts,* p. 175.
25. *Ibid.,* pp. 15–16.
26. *Ibid.,* pp. 22–26.
27. *Ibid.,* p. 30.
28. *Ibid.,* p. 4.
29. *Ibid.,* pp. 40–41.
30. *Ibid.,* p. 14.
31. *Ibid.,* p. 135.
32. *Ibid.,* p. 145.
33. *Ibid.,* p. 132.
34. A. C. Swinburne, "William Blake" in *Complete Works,* Bonchurch Edn., ed. Edmund Gosse and T. J. Wise (London, 1926), X, 24.
35. J. M. Whistler, *The Gentle Art of Making Enemies* (New York, 1953), p. 144.
36. *The Symbolist Movement in Literature,* pp. 74–75.
37. *Studies in Seven Arts,* pp. 64–65.
38. *Ibid.,* p. 238.
39. *Ibid.,* pp. 265–66.
40. *Ibid.,* p. 194.
41. *Plays, Acting and Music,* pp. 300–02.
42. *Ibid.,* pp. 310–11.
43. Graham Hough, *The Last Romantics,* p. 185.
44. *Dramatis Personae,* pp. 343–44.
45. *Cities,* London: 1903, p. v.
46. *Ibid.,* pp. vi–vii.
47. See Richard Jennings, "Arthur Symons," *New Statesman and Nation,* XXIX (February 17, 1945), 111.
48. *Cities of Italy* (London, 1907), p. vii.
49. *Cities,* p. 184.
50. *Ibid.,* p. 96.
51. T. S. Eliot, *The Sacred Wood* (London, 1920), pp. 2–5. The essay on *Antony and Cleopatra* to which Eliot refers is included in *Studies in the Elizabethan Drama* (New York, 1919), pp. 1–20.
52. *Dramatis Personae,* p. 87.
53. Quoted Edmund Blunden, *The Examiner Examined* (London, 1928), p. 10.
54. G. F. Tatham, *The Letters of William Blake Together With His Life,* ed. A. G. B. Russell (London, 1959).
55. Alexander Gilchrist, *The Life of William Blake: Pictor Ignotus* (London, 1863).
56. A. C. Swinburne, *Complete Works,* Bonchurch Edition, X, 51–352.

57. W. M. Rossetti, ed., *The Collected Works of William Blake* (London, 1874).

58. Edwin Ellis and W. B. Yeats, eds., *The Works of William Blake* (London, 1893).

59. *Ibid.*, I, x.

60. Virginia Moore, *The Unicorn*, p. 85.

61. W. B. Yeats, *Essays and Introductions*, p. 114.

62. *Ibid.*, p. 116.

63. "Romani Rai," unpub. MS in Symons Collection, Princeton University Library, n.d.

64. Later collected in *Essays and Introductions* under the title "William Blake and His Illustrations to the *Divine Comedy*."

65. *Collected Works*, I, 165.

66. *Ibid.*, III, 7–11.

67. *Poetry and prose of William Blake*, ed. Geoffrey Keynes (London, 1930), p. 193.

68. *William Blake*, Travellers' Library (London, 1928), p. 67.

69. Hazard Adams, *Blake and Yeats: The Contrary Vision* (New York, 1955), p. 47.

70. *William Blake*, p. 25.

71. *Ibid.*, p. 27.

72. *Ibid.*, p. 73.

73. *Ibid.*, p. 65.

74. *Ibid.*, p. 130.

75. *Ibid.*, p. 66.

76. *Collected Works*, II, 192–93.

77. *William Blake*, p. 86.

78. *Ibid.*, p. 198.

79. *Plays, Acting and Music*, p. viii.

80. *Spiritual Adventures*, p. 189. Cf. *Confessions: A Study in Pathology* (New York, 1930), p. 45.

81. See p. 78.

82. In an unpublished essay in the Symons Collection at Princeton, Symons describes the genesis of *Spiritual Adventures*, indicating who his models were for the various studies. He notes that Esther Kahn was based on a Jewish actress he had met in the East End of London, whom he described more fully in another unpublished essay ("Impressions," Symons Collection, Princeton University Library, n.d.); Seaward Lackland he insists is pure invention; and Daniel Roserra is modeled on himself, while in the woman of the story, "Livia," there are traces of what was once enigmatical and passionate in a "wonderful girl, of mixed blood, like mine, who was my mistress for many years" (i.e., Lydia), and also "of a married woman, whose temperament was totally different from the other's" (Rhoda?).

Peter Waydelin, so Symons notes, was inspired by both Beardsley and Toulouse Lautrec, while in the study itself he had endeavored to give "a morbid analysis of diseased nerves and of a depraved imagination." Symons also comments: "Waydelin accepted his fate because his existence had turned back upon him in the invariable way of those who have failed in achieving what they had set their hearts on doing." See Arthur Symons, "The Genesis of *Spiritual Adventures,*" Symons Collection, Princeton University Library, n.d.

83. *Spiritual Adventures,* pp. 160–61.

84. *Ibid.,* p. 163.

85. *Ibid.,* p. 171.

86. *Ibid.,* p. 175.

87. *Ibid.,* p. 185.

88. "The Genesis of *Spiritual Adventures.*" Here Symons also notes that the poem quoted on p. 109 was based on an incident described to him by Pachmann himself.

89. *Spiritual Adventures,* p. 32.

90. *Ibid.,* p. 97. Cf. Symons' description of himself in *Confessions: A Study in Pathology,* p. 9: "The small things do not exist for me, but how terribly a few things do. Rage consumes me if I do not possess their ultimate essence. As for all else, my mind is a happy blank, and I am generally supposed to be heartless, passionless, indifferent."

91. *Spiritual Adventures,* pp. 116–17.

92. See Roger Lhombreaud, *Arthur Symons,* pp. 186, 271, 322n.

93. *Collected Works,* II, 223.

94. "Music in Venice," *Saturday Review,* CVI (October 17, 1908), 480.

95. *Confessions: A Study in Pathology,* pp. 2–3.

96. Arthur Symons, ed., *Poems by John Clare* (London, 1908), p. 24.

97. *The Romantic Movement in English Poetry* (London, 1909), pp. 140–41.

98. *Confessions: A Study in Pathology,* p. 5.

Chapter Five

1. Jessie Conrad, *Joseph Conrad and His Circle* (New York, 1935), p. 153. Richard Jennings also comments on the trance-like state in which Symons seems to have existed at this time: "About the middle of the last World War [Symons] used to send me [fragments and plans for literary subjects prepared before his collapse] evidently supposing that they could be worked up into articles. His letters and talk gave me the impression that he had escaped into the past. One of his letters to me was written on the faded notepaper of his long-extinct review,

The Savoy." Richard Jennings, "Arthur Symons," *New Statesman and Nation*, XXXIX (February 17, 1945), 111.

2. Quoted Guy Deghy and Keith Waterhouse, *Café Royal* (London, 1955), pp. 149–50.

3. Sylvia Beach, *Shakespeare and Company* (New York, 1959), pp. 176–77.

4. William Rothenstein, *Men and Memories*, III, 305.

5. *Collected Works*, II, 269, III, 26, 27, 36, 68, 237, 239, 257.

6. *Ibid.*, II, 274–85, 286–92; III, 173–95, 138–64.

7. *Ibid.*, III, 248.

8. *Ibid.*, III, 293.

9. *Ibid.*, III, 268.

10. From Arthur Symons, "Sonnets," unpub. MS, Symons Collection, Princeton University Library, n.d.

11. Arnold B. Sklare, "Arthur Symons: An Appreciation of the Critic of Literature," *Journal of Aesthetics and Art Criticism*, IX (June, 1951), 319.

12. Lionel Johnson to Katherine Tynan, originally published in *The Dublin Review*, October 1907, reptd. Ezra Pound, "Introduction," *The Poetical Works of Lionel Johnson* (London, 1915), p. xii.

13. William Rothenstein, *Men and Memories*, I, 239.

14. Stanislaus Joyce, *My Brother's Keeper* (New York, 1958), p. 197.

15. Augustus John, "Fragment of an Autobiography: X," *Horizon*, VIII, no. 44 (1943), 139–40.

16. *Wanderings* (London, 1931), p. 87.

17. See Roger Lhombreaud, *Arthur Symons*, pp. 155–62.

18. *Collected Works*, II, 182. There is some confusion in the dating of this poem. In Symons' *Collected Works* "Amends to Nature" is dated "Poltescoe, July 24, 1909," but it was originally included in *Fool of the World and Other Poems* (1906). Could it be that Symons wished his readers to assume that this poem was his first coherent statement after madness, in which he reviewed his past from the vantage of restored mental health and accounted for his mental breakdown?

19. *Collected Works*, III, 301–33.

20. *Baudelaire: Prose and Poetry*, p. v.

22. "Mr. Henley's Poetry," *Fortnightly Review*, LII (August, 1892), 184.

23. *The Symbolist Movement in Literature*, p. 3.

24. *Figures of Several Centuries*, pp. 310–12.

25. *Baudelaire: Prose and Poetry*, p. vi. This passage provoked a scathing attack on Symons by T. S. Eliot, who maintained that Symons had made Baudelaire's religion appear rather "childish," little more than a "game of children dressing up and playing at grownups." *Essays Ancient and Modern* (London, 1936), p. 65.

26. *Baudelaire: Prose and Poetry,* pp. 115, 186. C. F. Charles Baudelaire, *Oeuvres Complètes,* ed. Y-G. le Dantec (Paris, 1958), pp. 96, 143.

27. *Ibid.,* p. 144.

28. *Baudelaire: Prose and Poetry,* p. 124.

29. In an article which appeared at approximately the same time as his translations from Baudelaire, Symons makes a direct comparison between the temperament of the French poet and his own. "Confessions," *The Two Worlds,* II, 5 (September, 1926), 27.

30. *Baudelaire: A Study,* p. 67.

31. *Ibid.,* pp. 84–85.

32. *Ibid.,* pp. 97–98.

33. See Roger Lhombreaud, *Arthur Symons,* pp. 231–32.

34. *Dramatis Personae,* p. 3.

35. *Ibid.,* pp. 1–2.

36. Augustus John, "Fragment of an Autobiography—X," *Horizon,* VIII, no. 44 (1943), 139.

37. *An Introduction to the Study of Browning,* p. 27.

38. *Dramatis Personae,* p. 11.

39. *Notes on Joseph Conrad with Some Unpublished Letters* (London, 1925), p. 14. It is interesting to compare this volume with Symons' essay on Conrad in *Dramatis Personae.* The two pieces are substantially the same, but the later version lays even greater stress on Conrad's passionate cynicism and spiritual depravity.

40. *Ibid.,* p. 16.

41. Jessie Conrad, *Joseph Conrad and his Circle,* p. 154.

42. *Ibid.*

43. *Studies in Strange Souls* (London, 1929), p. 22.

44. *Ibid.,* p. 32.

45. *Ibid.,* pp. 63–69.

46. "Thomas Hardy," *Encyclopaedia Britannica* (11th edn.), XI, 948.

47. *The Café Royal and Other Essays* (London, 1923), pp. 36–37.

48. *Baudelaire: A Study,* p. 54.

49. *Notes on Joseph Conrad with Some Unpublished Letters,* pp. 16, 30.

50. *Studies in Strange Souls,* p. 37.

51. *Eleonora Duse* (London, 1927), pp. 84–87.

52. T. Earle Welby, *Arthur Symons,* p. 66.

53. Actually Symons was not the sole author of the play, as an unpublished essay in the Symons Collection at Princeton makes clear:

After I had read "A Modern Idyll" it occurred to me to turn this rather revolting material into a One Act Play. I mentioned the fact to [Frank] Harris and to [George] Moore, who urged me to try my hand in a form which was novel to me. Just then I had not the faintest idea of how one begins to write a play, how one constructs it, how one sets one's figures in motion, and how one contrives the final climax. Night after night I went across to Moore's rooms, showing him the fragments I had composed, which he read and commented upon. We ended by collaborating. Moore refused to have his name put beside mine on the play-bill. On Friday, March 4, 1892, it was performed at the Royalty Theatre under the auspices of the Independent Theatre.

Arthur Symons, "Frank Harris," unpub. MS, Symons Collection, Princeton University Library, n.d.

54. See Roger Lhombreaud, *Arthur Symons,* pp. 203–14.

55. Arthur Waugh, *Tradition and Change* (London, 1919), pp. 109–10.

56. T. Earle Welby, *Arthur Symons,* p. 77.

57. Priscilla Thouless, *Modern Poetic Drama* (Oxford, 1934), pp. 134–35.

58. T. S. Eliot, *Poetry and Drama* (Cambridge, Mass.: 1951).

59. Priscilla Thouless, *Modern Poetic Drama,* p. 9.

60. Symons evidently modeled his dramas after Maeterlinck, whose expressive silences he found both affecting and moving. See *The Symbolist Movement in Literature,* pp. 84–93. For such drama to be theatrically effective the poetic language must be sufficiently exalted to command the audience's imaginative involvement, and the dialogue spoken by actors and actresses whose stage presence equals that of Eleonora Duse. Failing these—and Symons' plays are certainly not poetically moving—the result could hardly be other than disappointing.

61. *Tragedies* (London, 1916), pp. 1–85.

62. *Ibid.,* p. 77.

63. *Ibid.,* pp. 87–121.

64. *Ibid.,* pp. 123–51.

65. *The Toy Cart* (Dublin, 1919).

66. *Tristran and Iseult* (London, 1917).

67. *Confessions: A Study in Pathology,* p. 5.

68. See T. S. Eliot, *The Sacred Wood,* p. 4, where he praises Symons' criticism of the French Symbolists and suggests that he was responsible for bringing these writers to his notice at an important stage in his career; *The Letters of Ezra Pound,* ed. D. D. Paige (New York, 1950), p. 218, where in a letter to René Taupin in 1928 he admits that the French influence came into his work through Symons. Pound did not limit his praise of Symons to his work on the French Symbolists. In a recently published letter from Pound to Floyd Dell, sometime editor of the Friday Literary Review of the *Chicago Evening Post,* he wrote: "I wonder who are your gods. One has too many to

confess.—I find my sanity in Plato, Dante, Spinoza, Pater, Symons, Longinus. . . ." G. Thomas Tanselle, "Two Early Letters of Ezra Pound," *American Literature*, XXXIV, 1 (March, 1962), 118. For Yeats's appreciation of Symons, see pp. 56–71.

69. See David Hayman, *Joyce et Mallarmé* (Paris, 1956), I, 27–34; James S. Atherton, *The Books at the Wake* (New York, 1960), p. 49. See also Mary Colum, *Life and the Dream* (London, 1947), p. 121, where she notes that all the students of Joyce's time were great admirers of Symons.

70. Although Pound's name and Ford's appeared with Symons' as "contributing editors" of the magazine, only Symons contributed. *The Two Worlds* is the kind of journal one can well imagine Symons writing for. A literary quarterly "dedicated to the increase of the gaiety of nations," circulated privately among its 450 subscribers, it specialized in erotica and mild forms of pornography, including nasty articles on Oscar Wilde, parts of the then unpublished, unauthorized sections of *De Profundis*, innumerable Beardsleyesque illustrations, and examples of Symons' more lurid later writing. The magazine is exceedingly rare but the University of North Carolina has several numbers, all of which contain contributions from Symons.

See "Outlaws of Life," *The Two Worlds*, I, 1 (September, 1925), 5–28. (a one-act playlet); "Les Demoiselles de Bienfilâtre," *Ibid.*, I, no. 1 (September, 1925), 100–07 (translation from Villiers de l'Isle. Adam); "Notes on Toulouse Lautrec and His Autographs," *Ibid.*, I, no. 2 (December, 1925), 162–69; "Notes on Verlaine's Adventures and Sensations," *Ibid.*, I, no. 3 (March, 1926), 267–79 (a significant essay insofar as Symons here makes what appears to be his only reference to Verlaine's homosexual relationship with Rimbaud); "Parallelement," *Ibid.*, I, no. 3 (March, 1926), 281–302 (translation from Verlaine); "The Last Day of Don Juan," *Ibid.*, I, no. 4 (June, 1926), 500–15 (a one-act playlet); "Confessions," *Ibid.*, II, no. 5 (September, 1926), 27–34 (an autobiographical fragment not included in *Confessions: A Study in Pathology*); "Confessions," *Ibid.*, II, no. 6 (December, 1926), 113–22 (autobiographical fragment later included in *Confessions: A Study in Pathology* in a slightly revised form).

71. See "Barbara Roscorla's Child," *The Little Review*, IV, no. 6 (October, 1917), 25–36; "Bertha," *Ibid.*, IV, no. 11 (March, 1918), 52–53.

72. Stuart Gilbert, ed., *The Letters of James Joyce* (New York, 1957), p. 98.

73. Symons' review of *Chamber Music* appeared in *The Nation*, LXXIII (October 15, 1907), 432. He also included it in the Epilogue to *The Joyce Book*, ed. Herbert Hughes (London, 1933). The text from which I have quoted is Symons' typescript for the Epilogue. See Arthur

Symons, "Epilogue," Symons Collection, Princeton University Library, n.d., pp. 1–2.

74. *Ibid.*, p. 4.

75. A. L. S. Arthur Symons to James Joyce, June 19, 1914, "Joyce Collection," Cornell University Library.

76. Arthur Symons, "Epilogue," Symons Collection, Princeton University Library, n.d., pp. 5, 7.

77. *Ibid.*, p. 1.

78. *Ibid.*, pp. 4–5.

79. *The Café Royal and Other Essays*, p. 11.

80. *Ibid.*, p. 13.

81. *Ibid.*, p. 17.

82. "Some Makers of Modern Verse," *Forum*, LXVI (1921), 483–84.

83. Simon Jesty, "Arthur Symons," *Times Literary Supplement* (February 3, 1945), p. 57.

84. Symons' obituary in the *Times Literary Supplement* (February 3, 1945), p. 57, is typical. See also Richard Jennings' comment on Symons' status as a writer in his obituary for the *New Statesman and Nation*, part of which has been quoted on p. viii.

Chapter Six

1. "Mr. Arthur Symons," *Times Literary Supplement* (May 14, 1925), p. 330.

2. See Roger Lhombreaud, *Arthur Symons*, pp. 163–65.

3. Arthur Symons, "The Genius and Failure of Berlioz," *Saturday Review*, CVI (July 25, 1908), 110.

Selected Bibliography

To compile a complete bibliography of the writings of Arthur Symons is a major project in itself. Not only did Symons publish over fifty volumes in England and the United States, edit, translate or introduce some fifty more, but he also contributed hundreds of articles and reviews to periodicals in England, France, Belgium, Spain, and the United States, the greater part of them appearing during the 1890's and the early years of the twentieth century when he was a regular contributor to *The Star, The Athenaeum* and *The Saturday Review.*

Symons also had a habit of using previously published material in later work, sometimes in collections of essays reprinting whole articles without revision, sometimes revising them before reprinting, sometimes running two or more previously published pieces together, sometimes stringing together paragraphs from a number of different articles and interspersing them with additional comments and personal reminiscence, all of which adds considerable difficulty to the bibliographer's task.

A complete, annotated bibliography of Symons' writings and criticism of him is at present being prepared by *English Literature in Transition.* What follows is simply a list of Symons' most important volumes, which the reader may supplement by referring to the notes.

PRIMARY SOURCES

Collected Works of Arthur Symons. 9 vols. London: Martin Secker, 1924. Originally, Symons' *Collected Works* were supposed to include sixteen volumes, but only nine were published. (See the original announcement in *The Times Literary Supplement,* November, 26, 1925, p. 462, and Roger Lhombreaud's comment in *Arthur Symons,* p. 294.) The nine published volumes are as follows: I-III, *Poems;* IV, *William Blake;* V, *Spiritual Adventures;* VI-VII, *Tragedies;* VIII, *Studies in Two Literatures;* IX, *Studies in Seven Arts.* Because the *Collected Edition* is not complete and because the volumes which did appear were in some instances revised or cut, readers should consult original editions of Symons' work whenever possible.

An Introduction to the Study of Browning. London: Cassell and Co., 1886. New edition, revised and enlarged. London: J. M. Dent, 1906.

Days and Nights. London: Macmillan and Co., 1889.

Silhouettes. London: Elkin Mathews and John Lane, 1892. Second edition, revised with additions. London: Leonard Smithers, 1898.

London Nights. London: Leonard Smithers, 1895. Second edition, revised. London: Leonard Smithers, 1897.

Amoris Victima. London: Leonard Smithers, 1897.

Studies in Two Literatures. London: Leonard Smithers, 1897.

Aubrey Beardsley. London: The Unicorn Press, 1898. New edition, revised and enlarged. London: J. M. Dent, 1905.

Images of Good and Evil. London: William Heinemann, 1899.

The Symbolist Movement in Literature. London: William Heinemann, 1899. Revised edition. London: Archibald Constable, 1908.

The Loom of Dreams. Privately printed, 1901.

Poems. London: William Heinemann, 1901. Collected edition in 2 vols.

Cities. London: J. M. Dent, 1903.

London: A Book of Aspects. Privately printed, 1903.

Plays, Acting and Music. London: Duckworth and Co., 1903, Revised edition. London: Archibald Constable, 1909.

Studies in Prose and Verse. London: J. M. Dent, 1904.

A Book of Twenty Songs. London: J. M. Dent, 1905.

Spiritual Adventures. London: Archibald Constable, 1905.

The Fool of the World and Other Poems. London: William Heinemann, 1906.

Studies in Seven Arts. London: Archibald Constable, 1906. Revised edition. London: Archibald Constable, 1925.

Great Acting in English. Privately printed, 1907.

Cities of Italy. London: J. M. Dent, 1907.

William Blake. London: Archibald Constable, 1907.

Lyrics. Portland, Maine: T. B. Mosher, 1909.

The Romantic Movement in English Poetry. London: Archibald Constable, 1909.

Knave of Hearts. London: William Heinemann, 1913.

Figures of Several Centuries. London: Archibald Constable, 1916.

Tragedies. London: William Heinemann, 1916.

Cities and Sea-Coasts and Islands. London: Collins, 1917.

Colour Studies in Paris. London: Chapman Hall, 1917.

Tristran and Iseult. London: William Heinemann, 1917.

Studies in Elizabethan Drama. London: William Heinemann, 1919.

The Toy Cart. London: Maunsel, 1919.

Charles Baudelaire: A Study. London: Mathews, 1920.

Lesbia and Others Poems. New York: E. P. Dutton, 1920.

The Café Royal and Other Essays. London: Beaumont Press, 1923.
Dramatis Personae. Indianapolis: Bobbs Merrill, 1923.
Love's Cruelty. London: Martin Secker, 1923.
From Catullus: Chiefly Concerning Lesbia. London: Martin Secker, 1924.
Baudelaire: Prose and Poetry. London: John Lane, 1925.
Notes on Joseph Conrad with Some Unpublished Letters. London: Myers, 1925.
Parisian Nights. London: Beaumont Press, 1926.
Eleonora Duse. London: Elkin Mathews, 1927.
The Letters of Charles Baudelaire to His Mother. London: J. Rodker, 1928.
From Toulouse Lautrec to Rodin. London: John Lane, 1929.
Studies in Strange Souls. London: Charles J. Sawyer, 1929.
Confessions: A Study in Pathology. London: Jonathan Cape, 1930.
Mes Souvenirs. Eure, France: The Hours Press, 1930.
A Study of Oscar Wilde. London: Charles J. Sawyer, 1930.
A Study of Thomas Hardy. London: Charles J. Sawyer, 1930.
Jezebel Mort and Other Poems. London: William Heinemann, 1931.
Wanderings. London: J. M. Dent, 1931.
A Study of Walter Pater. London: Charles J. Sawyer, 1932.
Amoris Victima. Privately printed, 1940.

SECONDARY SOURCES

Although Symons' name is frequently referred to in literary histories and almost always in memoirs and reminiscences of the 1890's he has received less than his share of critical attention, there being only four published, book-length studies of him, three of which hardly merit serious consideration:

Blaikie-Murdoch, W. G. *Arthur Symons*. Edinburgh: J. & I. Gray, 1907. A sympathetic but hardly profound study; almost exclusively concerned with Symons' verse.

Lhombreaud, Roger. *Arthur Symons*. London: Unicorn, 1963. Most useful and informative account of Symons which has so far appeared. The emphasis, however, is on Symons the man rather than on Symons the writer, and so there is little about his place in the history of modern English literature. Moreover, the book is marred by incredible carelessness in matters of detail.

Welby, T. Earle. *Arthur Symons*. London: A. M. Philpot, 1924. Superficial account of Symons' achievement as a writer; adds little to understanding of the man or his significance as a writer.

Wildi, Max. *Arthur Symons als Kritiker der Literatur*. Anglistiche Forschungen, Heidelberg, 1929, Hft. 67. German doctoral dissertation on Symons as critic; understates his interest in Verlaine and the French Symbolists, but is nonetheless good in so far as it draws attention to Symons' immense debt to Pater.

Baugh, Edward. *A Critical Study of the Writings of Arthur Symons.* Unpub. Ph.D. dissertation, Manchester University, 1964. Elaborates some of the points made by Frank Kermode in *Romantic Image* (see below), and is especially good on Symons and the image of the dance.

————. "Arthur Symons and 'The Symphony of Snakes,'" *English Literature in Transition,* VII, 4 (1964), 228–29. Reply to John M. Munro's article on "The Symphony of Snakes" published in the same journal (see below), noting that his remarks would have been enhanced by reference to Symons' poem "The Andante of Snakes."

————. "Arthur Symons, Poet: A Centenary Tribute," *A Review of English Literature,* VI, 3 (1965). Brief but excellent review of Symons' poetry.

Beckson, Karl & Munro, John M. "Letters from Arthur Symons to James Joyce: 1904–1932," *James Joyce Quarterly,* IV, 2 (1967), 91–101. Account of the Symons-Joyce relationship, revealing Symons' role in helping Joyce find publishers for his early work.

Ellmann, Richard, ed. *The Symbolist Movement in Literature* by Arthur Symons. New York: Dutton, 1958. Has some interesting discussion of Symons' most important book, but misses many of its significant implications by isolating it from the rest of his work.

Fletcher, Ian. "Explorations and Recoveries II," *London Magazine,* VII, 6 (June, 1960), 49–60. Account of Symons' close association with Yeats, especially in relation to their handling of the image of the dance.

Gribble, Francis. "The Prose of Mr. Arthur Symons," *Fortnightly Review,* XC (July, 1908), 127–36. Best of early articles on Symons; draws attention to the supreme importance of Symons' early Methodist upbringing in relation to his work.

Irvine, Peter. *A Biographical Study of Arthur Symons.* Unpub. Ph.D. dissertation, Columbia University, 1965. Good biographical survey and an account of the reception of his major works, but has only general critical comment on the works.

Kermode, Frank. *Romantic Image.* London: Kegan Paul, 1957. An excellent chapter on Symons emphasizes his role as an intermediary between Arnold and Pater on the one hand, and Eliot, Pound, and T. E. Hulme on the other.

More, Paul Elmer. "Arthur Symons: The Two Illusions." *Shelburne Essays.* First Series. Boston: Houghton Mifflin, 1907. Survey of Symons' poetry tracing Symons' growing disillusionment.

Munro, John M. "Arthur Symons as Poet: Theory and Practice,"

English Literature in Transition, VI, 4 (1963), 212–22. Survey of Symons' achievement as a poet with particular emphasis on *Silhouettes* and *London Nights.*

―――. "Arthur Symons, 'The Symphony of Snakes,' and the Development of the Romantic Image," *English Literature in Transition,* VII, 3 (1964), 143–45. Publication of one of Symons' notebooks with commentary, suggesting that Symons was obscurely aware of the nature of the "romantic image" long before he became intimate with Yeats. (See above, a reply to this article by Edward Baugh.)

―――. "Arthur Symons and W. B. Yeats: The Quest for Compromise," *Dalhousie Review,* XL, 2 (1965), 137–52. An account of the relationship between Symons and Yeats.

―――. "Arthur Symons's Mental Breakdown: Bolgora, 1908," *Notes and Queries,* XIV, 7, new series (1967), 250. Text of a letter to Richard Hutton written immediately before Symons' breakdown.

Sklare, Arnold B. "Arthur Symons: An Appreciation of The Critic of Literature," *Journal of Aesthetics and Art Criticism,* IX (June, 1951), 319–31. Good, brief analysis of Symons' importance as a critic, more perceptive and certainly superior to Wildi's dissertation on the same subject.

Temple, Ruth Z. "Arthur Symons." *The Critic's Alchemy.* New York: Twayne, 1953. Excellent survey of Symons' relations with the French Symbolists; very sound and admirably documented.

Thouless, Priscilla. "Arthur Symons." *Modern Poetic Drama.* Oxford: Blackwell, 1934. Discussion of Symons' achievements in verse drama viewed against his contemporaries' exercises in the genre. Perhaps an over-generous appreciation of this aspect of Symons' work.

Index

ARTHUR SYMONS